Reading Lives

WORKING-CLASS CHILDREN
AND LITERACY LEARNING

Deborah Hicks

FOREWORD BY JANE MILLER

Teachers College, Columbia University
New York and London

D0057566

Published by Teachers College Press, 1234 Amsterdam Avenue, New York, NY 10027

Copyright © 2002 by Teachers College, Columbia University

Portions of Chapter 5 are adapted from "Literacies and Masculinities in the Life of a Young Working-Class Boy," by Deborah Hicks, 2001, *Language Arts, 78*, pp. 217–226. Adapted with permission.

Portions of Chapter 6 are adapted from "Self and Others in Bakhtin's Early Philosophical Essays: Prelude to a Theory of Prose Consciousness," by Deborah Hicks, 2000, *Mind, Culture, and Activity, 7*, pp. 227–242. Adapted with permission.

Library of Congress Cataloging-in-Publication Data

Hicks, Deborah.
    Reading lives : working-class children and literacy learning / Deborah Hicks ; foreword by Jane Miller.
      p. cm. — (Language and literacy series)
    Includes bibliographical references (p.) and index.
    ISBN 0-8077-4150-7 (cloth : alk. paper) — ISBN 0-8077-4149-3 (pbk. : alk. paper)
     1. Working class—Education—United States—Case studies. 2. Children—Books and reading—Case studies. I. Title. II. Language and literacy series (New York, N.Y.)

    LC5051 .H53 2001
    372.1826'23—dc21   2001041573

ISBN 0-8077-4149-3 (paper)
ISBN 0-8077-4150-7 (cloth)

Printed on acid-free paper

Manufactured in the United States of America

09   08   07   06   05   04   03   02   8 7 6 5 4 3 2 1

For my mother
Betty Louise Hicks

Contents

Foreword

LITERATURE OCCUPIES A PARADOXICAL position in recent studies of children acquiring literacy. It is at once the means and the target of the process of learning to read and write in school, yet it is almost wholly absent from the research itself as a source of either understanding or illumination. With great subtlety, Deborah Hicks addresses that paradox: first, by setting her long-term study of Laurie and Jake, two working-class children growing up in the small-town Mid-Atlantic region of the United States, within and alongside her own story of growing up and the stories a clutch of writers—Annie Ernaux, Janet Frame, Mike Rose, among others—have told about their early schooldays. In addition, she invokes the insistence of the Russian theorist Mikhail Bakhtin on the moral and emotional significance of our earliest uses of language. Language is not simply a communicative tool; it is imbued with, drenched by, the particular relations and feelings that children experience as they learn language and as they move on from there to develop literacy. Learning is marked by those traces, and, as Hicks puts it, "What is required for critical literacy teaching is not just the right kinds of discourses, but the right kinds of relationships." To understand the difficulties some children experience in their transition from home to school, Hicks suggests that we may gain greater insight from philosophers of literature—Martha Nussbaum, for example, or Iris Murdoch—than from those educational psychologists who condemn one of Hicks's children to the consequences of a diagnosis of ADD (attention deficit disorder), while the other child is made responsible for losing by the second year of school the headstart offered him by his assured role as a talented child in his family.

There is delicacy in the detail of these two young lives, watched over several years as initial optimism about school achievement collapses into confusion and pain. The readings Hicks makes of these children and their

families and of literary accounts and the theoretical perspectives she brings *
to such accounts allow her to argue for new forms of research as well as
new approaches to the schooling of working-class children. She invites
us as readers of her narratives, her evidence, and her speculation to
consider Nussbaum's injunction to hover "in thought and imagination
around the enigmatic complexities of the seen particular." Why should
educational inquiries conform to the dispassionate language of the social
sciences, Hicks asks, rather than to the passionate assembling of concrete
particulars: of children's relations with others and with the occasionally
insurmountable obstacles to a smooth translation from those into what
is required by school? Hicks argues for research texts that are generically
hybrid and open to the reader's participation in the struggle and the
difficulties of understanding another's experience. Teachers have to face
that sort of challenge, and the need for knowledge about the children
they teach, if they are to enlist their students into successful learning.
Generalized or stereotypical accounts of how class and race and gender
may articulate with children's coming to terms with the institutions and
procedures of school must be resisted in favor of the long haul, patient
listening, imaginative sympathy, and attention to the particular, the un-
predicted. It is the duty of those who support teachers and schools through
their research and writing to argue for that process and to reject short-
cut descriptions or explanations of success and failure. Deborah Hicks's
book makes a moving plea for the serious business of research into how
young children learn best.

Jane Miller
Professor Emeritus in Education, University of London

Acknowledgments

I AM DEEPLY GRATEFUL for the support of friends and colleagues throughout the writing of this book. Jane Miller has been an especially important reader of this work as it emerged over the past 2 years. She provided invaluable feedback on an earlier version of the manuscript. Mike Rose and Tim Lensmire have each helped me sort through some particularly difficult moments of writing. Jim Gee has been a friend and mentor for more than a decade and was instrumental in helping me to shape a theoretical framework for this research. Finally, Bob Hampel has helped me through many a time when the work of writing this book seemed bigger than I was.

This project developed while I was teaching at the University of Delaware, and many dialogues with colleagues there contributed to the project. Eugene Matusov, Kathy Schultz, and Tony Whitson offered especially valuable insights. Hope Longwell-Grice, then a doctoral student, provided important assistance with the research in its first year. A science education colleague, Nancy Brickhouse, collaborated on one part of the study in its third and final year. Three amazing primary-grade teachers, who cannot be named for reasons of confidentiality, graciously opened the doors of their classrooms to me and offered wisdom and analytical insight as the research project evolved.

At the University of Cincinnati, where I completed the writing of this book, doctoral students in the Literacy Program provided helpful feedback on an early version of this book. Tammy Schwartz and Karen Titsworth have been especially important critical readers and supportive colleagues.

My deepest gratitude is extended to Jake and Laurie and their families, for allowing me to see and feel the particulars of their lives. My commitment to them and caring has shaped the pages of this book, helping me to find the right words to express educational theory and research.

The early parts of this project were funded through a Small Research Grant from the Spencer Foundation. I am indebted to the Spencer Foundation for their support of my research and writing over the years. I am responsible for the research itself and any intellectual ideas resulting from it.

1

Overview

THE THEORETICAL UNDERPINNINGS OF this book came from my readings of literature and philosophy; the empirical descriptions and analyses, from my relationships with two children. That the sources of inspiration for this book are rooted in lived relationships and fictional lives is fitting for its purpose. One of the arguments threaded throughout the chapters that follow concerns the ways in which students' engagements with literacies—or institutional modes of talking, reading, and writing—are connected with their own histories, formed with others whom they value and love. Students' searches for social belonging are as much a part of learning in school as anything that might be described as cognitive or even discursive. Sometimes missing in research discourses about literacy learning are the histories that shape connections with school and workplace literacies. This is partly because educational inquiry has been largely influenced by social scientific discourses, in which the focus is on generalized descriptions and analyses. The intimate perspectives that one might find in the discourses of the novel are more distanced from the writing of literacy research texts and the shaping of educational theory. Throughout this book, I attempt to write what Jane Miller (1996) refers to as *hybrid* theoretical discourses. Narrative histories of lives are interwoven with essayist commentary and critical reflection. My choice of writing forms is connected to my commitment to articulating a theory of literacy learning that has the particularity of social relations at its center.

Because of these commitments, the chapters that follow draw on mixed genres. Narrative histories of children's lives and engagements with literacies, interpretive readings of other histories of engagement with literacies, and essayist reflections on educational theory and practice form part of a hybrid text. The narratives read and composed in this book are focused on how working-class students engage with middle-class literacies and how those engagements are interwoven with relations with others. In Chapters 4 and 5, I tell the stories of how two working-class students, Jake and Laurie, participated in literacy practices as they moved between the social worlds of home and school in kindergarten through second grade. The histories of these two young children are framed by reflective chapters that also consider narratives written by adults (e.g., educational scholars, literary writers) looking back on their experiences growing up in the working classes. Narrative readings of my own childhood in a rural, blue-collar setting become part of the considerations of working-class students' life experiences in terms of historicity and cultural complexity. I allow the particularity of feeling and intimate relations to penetrate those composed texts, just as I argue reflectively that feeling and valuing are integral to what it means to know. I argue in Chapter 6, drawing on some essays by philosopher Martha Nussbaum, that feeling can guide teachers and researchers to knowing in ways that are more fully responsive to the particulars of how working-class students engage with middle-class literacy practices. Students' engagements with school and institutional literacies are caught up with their searches for love and social belonging. Should not relations of feeling and valuing therefore be included in the ways in which literacy educators shape their practices and theories?

In her fictional story "The Member of the Wedding," Carson McCullers writes of the adolescent longings of a central character, Frankie (a.k.a., F. Jasmine). In a story taking place over several days in Frankie's life, McCullers writes about some of the changes happening as Frankie and those closest to her prepare for her brother's wedding. Set in a southern town in the midst of summer, the story chronicles the slow, unfolding particulars of Frankie's responses to the changes occurring as she encounters new experiences and feelings, some tied to an emerging fantasy that she will join the wedding couple as a third "member." As the story evolves, it immerses readers in the detail of lived and felt moments:

> She stood before the mirror and she was afraid. It was the summer of fear, for Frankie, and there was one fear that could be figured in arithmetic with paper and pencil at the table. This August she was twelve and five-sixths years old. She was five feet five and three quarter inches tall, and she wore a number seven shoe. In the past year she had grown four inches, or at least that was what she judged. Already the hateful little summer children hollered to her: "Is it cold up there?" And the comments of grown people made Frankie shrivel on her heels. If she reached her height on her eighteenth birthday, she had five and one-sixth growing years ahead of her. Therefore, according to mathematics and unless she could somehow stop herself, she

would grow to be over nine feet tall. And what would be a lady who is over nine feet high? She would be a Freak. (McCullers, 1946/1987, p. 271)

As this fictional text evolves, it begins to elaborate a central theme in Frankie's thinking and action: her search for social identity and connection—a "we of me" in relation with others. Just days before the wedding, Frankie reflects on how a new sense of social belonging has changed her feelings about herself in relation to the southern community in which her childhood history emerged. Her valuing of particular others is changing who she is; her longing for social connection is shaping the *what* and *how* of her learning in social worlds extending beyond her immediate family and loved ones:

Yesterday, and all the twelve years of her life, she had only been Frankie. She was an *I* person who had to walk around and do things by herself. All other people had a *we* to claim, all others except her. When Berenice said *we*, she meant Honey and Big Mama, her lodge, or her church. The *we* of her father was the store. All members of clubs have a *we* to belong to and to talk about. The soldiers in the army can say *we*, and even the criminals on chain-gangs. But the old Frankie had had no *we* to claim, unless it would be the terrible summer *we* of her and John Henry and Berenice—and that was the last *we* in the world she wanted. Now all this was suddenly over with and changed. There was her brother and the bride, and it was as though when first she saw them something she had known inside of her: *They are the we of me.* And that was why it made her feel so queer, for them to be away in Winter Hill while she was left all by herself; the hull of the old Frankie left there in the town alone. (p. 291)

As working-class children entering a school system modeled after middle-class values and practices, Laurie and Jake wanted desperately to find a *we of me* in school. When school practices did not afford them spaces for belonging, Jake and Laurie turned to other values and practices as points of identity and connection. Still, their engagements with school literacies were threaded even into their resistances, as these two young working-class children tried to figure out how they belonged in school. The stories I write of the literacy practices lived by Laurie and Jake are laced with pain as well as hope, as both children became readers and writers in a school setting that was sometimes distancing and sometimes embracing. Their histories as readers and writers are written with a commitment to viewing literacies as situated practices and relations in the world. Shaping those complex histories in part through narrative form allows the researcher to "see" and value things differently, in ways that come closer to the richly detailed compositions of a fiction writer. "To write in different ways is to live in different ways," argues Raymond Williams (1977). Across the stories and reflective essays in this book, I hope to write in such a way that the reader can see and feel the complex histories of working-class children's engagements with literacy practices and searches for love and belonging.

The history of the research project that led to this book takes me back to a particular time and place, and the personal and professional relationships formed as the project evolved. Having spent years studying how children engage with classroom discourses in urban, multiethnic classroom settings, I wanted to focus my research lens more narrowly on the literate engagements of children growing up in poor and working-class White families. I was concerned that much of the educational literature on the learning needs of working-class learners focused less on *class* than on ethnicity, a hidden message being that poor and working-class children are largely members of ethnic-minority families and neighborhoods. Though clearly there is an urgent need for research and advocacy among ethnically diverse and language-minority students, many of the nation's poor and working-class families are White. Their treatment in school systems and in society at large can be oppressively hegemonic in ways that are submerged because of the hidden nature of class consciousness in the United States. More visible in nations like Great Britain, where class issues are talked about, researched, and theorized, class differences are often glossed over in the United States, with the end result that White poor and working-class children are viewed negatively but without cultural sensitivity. Central to this book is the argument that White working-class children often experience painful cultural dissonance in middle-class classrooms, and that teachers and researchers need to strive for critical practices that address the varying diversities they might encounter—those involving relations of ethnicity, race, gender, *and* class.

That I took on this particular research focus is a reflection both of my childhood history in a rural, blue-collar family and community, and of my later years of immersion in a community of cultural literacy scholars. Having grown up in a largely working-class community, I was as an adult researcher sensitive to portrayals of the learning histories of children from similar backgrounds—children like those depicted in Shirley Brice Heath's (1983) portrayal of the White working-class community she called Roadville. As I read descriptions like this one, I found myself nodding my head at familiar practices and wondering whether other educators were concerned about children like those in Heath's study or were perhaps also nodding their heads with childhood recollections. I do not think that modern communities, rural or urban, are fixed in terms of class identities.

Working-class families participate in yuppie practices, buying coffee grinders and juicers even as they talk and value in ways much more typical of blue-collar life. My own family experiences were mixed in this way. My family had middle-class aspirations and pushed education strongly. Still, there were unique struggles I faced as a learner who later encountered academic discourses and values that initially seemed foreign and dislocating. As I read cultural literacy studies that considered children from varied communities, I found myself especially inspired by questions about how other working-class children dealt with middle-class discourses as young students and what challenges they faced as learners. I felt that there were many holes in cultural literacy research literatures when it came to questions about class and gender. I turned to the writings of British educators, and often to feminists, to find theory and research that talked explicitly about social-class and gender differences and their educational significance. However, most of the work described in this book comes out of field-based studies in which I lived and researched the day-to-day realities of working-class children's struggles within a middle-class educational system.

That work is informed by particular histories and relationships. As I sought and found an educational setting in which I could spend 3 years researching this topic, I had the good fortune of being introduced to an amazing kindergarten teacher, Mrs. Thompson.* Together, we formed a research relationship that made space for me in her classroom as a researcher-teacher and that helped me get to know children and their families. Mrs. Thompson's kindergarten classroom was situated in a predominately White working-class neighborhood in a small town in the Mid-Atlantic region, not too far from a regional urban center. Streets lined with small, wood-framed houses and grassy front lawns made up the neighborhood immediately surrounding the school where she taught; most families living close to the school were of blue-collar or working-poor socioeconomic status. Children from a nearby urban, largely African American, community were also members of the kindergarten classroom in which this study had its beginnings. Spending 1 day each week as a participant in the life of this kindergarten classroom, I initially selected six children who lived in the nearby working-class neighborhood surrounding the primary school, with the intention of observing and documenting the K–2 learning histories of all six students. I wrote fieldnotes

---

*All names used throughout this book are pseudonyms, including those of the classroom teachers involved in this study. Although Mrs. Thompson and other teachers contributed substantially to the research understandings of the two children in the study, we collectively felt that revealing the teachers' identities would compromise the children's anonymity.

documenting their classroom activities, visited the children at home, and photocopied samples of their writings and drawings. As this research evolved and I followed the children into first and then second grade, it became clear that what I was looking for was an intimate perspective on how young children in working-class communities engage with school literacy practices. Such a perspective could best be garnered through close observations of individual children, and through a kind of research that entailed relationships developed over time.

That my research lens became focused on Jake and Laurie, two young members of Mrs. Thompson's classroom, is in part a reflection of advocacy and in part a reflection of the fact that some families were more interested in engaging in dialogues with an outsider about their children. Jake's family welcomed me into their home with open arms from the beginnings of this project, and this created a vibrant opportunity for dialogue about home and school learning. His family allowed me to experience richly the forms of life he lived as a young boy at home. Laurie's family also welcomed me into their home, though the reason for focusing on Laurie's K–2 learning experiences arose out of my concerns for her academic difficulties, concerns shared by her family members. When it became clear in first grade that Laurie was not making it in school, I began adopting a somewhat different research role with her. I became Laurie's tutor, as Laurie and I tried to figure out together how she was going to learn to read and write in school. By the time Laurie and Jake were in the second grade, my research lens was focused exclusively on them. The administration at their K–2 school generously agreed to keep the children together in the same classrooms, so that I could observe both of them on the same research day—1 day per week from kindergarten through second grade. The research contributions of their classroom teachers became an important part of the research understandings and histories that are chronicled in Chapters 4 and 5.

The forms of data collection and analysis that emerged as most appropriate to this project reflect both traditional and nontraditional methods of qualitative inquiry. As with other examples of classroom-based qualitative inquiry, I drew on multiple sources of documentation to record and later rework my interpretive readings of classroom activity. On classroom research days, I wrote observational fieldnotes, and I also participated in instructional activities as a support for children and their teachers. I was not viewed by the children as a regular teacher, but neither did I attempt to step into the role of peer or family member. Children referred to me using my last name, as was the norm in the school for addressing teaching adults. My classroom observations included videotaping of selected classroom events; audiotaping of children's conversations, oral narratives, and bookreadings; photocopying of artifacts, such as writing samples and drawings; and audiotaping of teacher–researcher dialogues. Classroom fieldnotes, supplemented by audiotaped or videotaped segments of oral language, were reworked into narrative form as soon as possible after a classroom research day. Home visits were written in narrative form only, since during home visits I did not record ongoing fieldnotes. Finally, in the summers following the children's kindergarten and first-grade years, their teachers and I jointly constructed (with the assistance of a research assistant, Hope Longwell-Grice) a review of their progress the year before. These teacher–researcher dialogues drew from oral inquiry processes developed by Patricia Carini (e.g., 1982) for use among class-room teachers. We used teacher–researcher dialogues to construct learn-ing biographies of Laurie and Jake, in hopes that these child review texts would help their families and upcoming teachers—those most concerned with meeting the children's educational needs. A learning portrait com-posed for Jake in the summer following his kindergarten year is included in the Appendix. This portrait was the result of 2 days of collaborative dialogue and analysis.

The hope that this long-term research project would also engender advocacy for the children, their families, and their teachers was muted by the larger educational and societal constraints that all involved experi-enced. Educators concerned about issues of social justice often express their hopefulness that things can change for poor and working-class chil-dren—that more typical patterns of hegemonic and oppressive relations in society at large can be changed through education. For instance, in his book about literacy education for working-class students, Patrick Finn (1999) argues for a liberating pedagogy that draws on progressive theories and methods. What works for children at the upper end of the economic ladder, where parents send their children to Montessori kindergartens and insist on inquiry-based learning, he argues, can and should also be liberating for working-class children. Jeanne Brady (1995) similarly argues for pedagogics aimed at social justice and access to literacies.

Making this *happen*, however, is another matter. Like most working-class students in the United States, Jake and Laurie attended a school that embraced traditional values and teaching practices. Even though their individual teachers looked beyond that system to alternative educational practices, their teaching was framed within the constraints of an institution and wider system. The hope that this research project could be used as a mechanism for educational change, even if only for the two children in the study (with the hope that those results could then *later* be generalized), was often at odds with practices and values that framed research and day-to-day teaching. The extensive child review texts, for instance, seemed to have little long-term impact on the two children's school lives. These "thick assessments" were embedded in practices and expectations that did not make pedogogical space for them. Beyond kindergarten, teachers at the school attended by Laurie and Jake felt pressured to make sure that children were meeting grade-level expectations in subjects like literacy and mathematics. From first grade onward, Jake and Laurie struggled with educational practices that were difficult and often distancing for them. This became increasingly frustrating for them, their families, and the researcher and teachers who worked hard to make things different.

That this book is thus primarily a recounting of histories of working-class lives, with a special focus on young children's engagements with literacies, is perhaps both its strength and its weakness. The wider aim of creating liberatory pedagogies for poor and working-class children may for the moment take second place to the aim of understanding some particular learning histories. The intimate and historicized perspective that I take on learning in this book may be a small step toward collectively figuring out how researchers, teachers, and community grassroots leaders can help education be liberatory for poor and working-class children. Looking closely at language and learning processes over time, seeing things up close and personally, may engender more subtle ways of changing hegemonic relations in public schools. If constructing hybrid forms of educational research writing also contributes something to this change process, then I would gladly accept the responsibility of having done research that only partly met its aims for social justice.

Crucial to the inquiry processes that undergird the narratives and essayist reflections in this book is the sense of time, or historicity, that helped constitute the project. Lengthy periods of time doing field-based studies and scholarly inquiry do not necessarily mesh with the more contemporary demands of academic life. Scholarly research and advocacy in the current era of fast capitalism and "hard" outcomes or products are shaped by these wider social and economic contingencies. Images of field-based research extending over a period of years can quickly become replaced by images of shorter-term projects that generate more immediate results—be they textual products such as refereed journal articles or up-ward changes in kids' test scores. The sense of time as it unfolds in a slow, everyday sense of lived experience can easily become lost, or at least distanced, amid the research practices that define cultural literacy studies. Ironically, the very strength of models of research that emphasize cultural processes is that they allow the researcher to live and feel the particulars of the social practices and relations lived by the subjects of inquiry. An example that again comes to mind is Heath's (1982, 1983) study of the *ways with words* of neighboring communities in the Piedmont.

Its focus on everyday life, and on the ways in which everyday life was shaped along spatial and temporal dimensions, was crucial to its importance for the field of cultural literacy research. Heath's later efforts to advocate for educational change were embedded in her understanding of cultural particulars, garnered through a decade of research. Outside of such historicity, this seminal literacy research project would have lost an important part of its epistemological force.

Such historicized research is becoming more difficult to justify amid changing institutional practices. Sadly so, for what if certain kinds of literacy practices require the specificity of lived time to comprehend, much less change, through theorizing, research, and advocacy? Central to my project were the ways in which a rich understanding of the lives of Laurie and Jake required the research dimension of historicity. Their biographies as learners would have been narrowly composed had I known them for only a year; the complex weaving of gender, social class, and literacy in their lives would have been seen in much more shallow ways. The slow, evolving nature of lived time is part of what enables or constitutes cultural literacy research, and perhaps even critical literacy research if it is to be more responsively constructed. This kind of historicity is most richly articulated, I argue in this book, through a rhetorical engagement with narratives.

As my research study of Jake and Laurie evolved over a 3-year period, and for a period of time extending beyond those field-based studies, I was also reading across disciplines such as education, psychology, philosophy, and the interdisciplinary nexus of scholarship that draws on feminist theory and practice. Initially trained as a sociolinguist, I took as my starting point the study of language practices. I searched across disciplines for work that would help me understand how children use language to negotiate identities and knowledge in the cultural worlds in which they come to be and know. As I became a researcher focused on studies of how language practices, or *discourses*, mediate these social becomings and knowings, I began drawing on the emerging field of sociocultural psychology. Sociocultural theorists working in education and psychology had created an interdisciplinary field of study that often viewed the work of Vygotsky (e.g., van der Veer & Valsiner, 1994; Vygotsky, 1934/1986) as a starting point. I, too, was drawn to Vygotsky's work, and especially to the importance he attributed to studies of language. In the theories of learning developed among scholars aligning themselves with cultural-historical and activity theory (CHAT) frameworks, language practices were viewed as central to how culturally specific knowledge is constructed. Discourses have been depicted in such literatures as symbolic, cultural practices that are part of a toolkit of thinking and action for individuals and social groups (Bruner, 1996; Wells, 1996; Wertsch, 1991). These metaphors capture the ways in which the discourses particular to communities, classrooms, and cultures shape how children know.

At the same time, I found myself drawn to another body of work, one that sometimes seemed far removed from the increasingly popular sociocultural learning theories in education and psychology. While sociocultural theorists were writing about how discourses mediate children's learning, feminists such as Valerie Walkerdine were creating an interdisciplinary body of scholarship that critiqued mainstream psychology (see Henriques, Hollway, Urwin, Venn, & Walkerdine, 1984; Walkerdine, 1988, 1990). Scholars writing *critical psychology* theory and research also viewed language practices as a focal point for their inquiries. However, the lenses used to reflect on social and cultural discourses were typically quite different. Feminist and critical psychologists drew upon interdisciplinary fields and often poststructuralist theories of language in ways that brought studies of power relations and subjectivities overtly into studies of learning. Becoming a subject amid material relations (e.g., economic relations; relations of class, gender, race) was emphasized in critical psychology. This more overt emphasis on what Walkerdine and Lucey (1989) describe as the *politics of subjectivity* seemed well suited to studies of children's class and gender identities, and the politics of learning in relation to them. However, I struggled with the poststructuralist frameworks that have so strongly influenced feminist and critical psychology. These seemed alien to me. My initial reactions when I read these often abstract discussions ranged from curiosity, to excitement, to repulsion. To appropriate some language from fiction writer Flannery O'Connor (1971/1998), I think I would have described writing in critical psychology as: Brilliant, but it doesn't make a grain of sense.

I think of those struggles with theory as themselves indicative of how meaningful the insights from critical psychology are. As I think back to my upbringing in a family strongly influenced by southern values and discourse practices, a scene comes to mind. It is from one of many visits to the larger city where my mother's extended family lived. Sitting out on a screened back porch, sipping iced tea and sharing stories and gossip, family members engaged in the slow, deliberate speech that is so typical of life downhome. Those long pauses and simple, declarative utterances reflected a certain identity. You had better not sound highfalutin like some fast-talking lawyer from the city. The sometimes difficult, abstract language of poststructuralist theory struck me as divorced from lived and felt realities, even as critical psychologists seemed to want to tell their readers about subjects and material relations in the world. It is when theory becomes distanced from what we perceive as our lived realities that it starts to lose its power for us as readers. It took many readings and rereadings of the work of critical and feminist psychologists before the languages used to evoke the interplay of knowledge, material practices, and identities began to be powerful languages of description for me. It is possible to live and value more than one subjectivity. A kind of hybrid voice was emerging that I now see as extremely powerful.

As this work evolved, I also found myself increasingly interested in reading philosophy. It wasn't so much mainstream Anglo European philosophy that sparked my interest, but a small group of philosophers who write about the connections of literature to philosophical inquiry, and the role of literary metaphors in thinking about experience. I count among those influential philosophers writers such as Iris Murdoch, Martha Nussbaum, Raymond Williams, and, most importantly, Mikhail Bakhtin. My readings and appropriations of their work have been selective and transformative. For instance, I found in Nussbaum's writings guidance for thinking about how literary texts can help engage readers with particular kinds of philosophical questions. Some of these questions are ones I also found critical for studies of literacy and, more generally, studies of learning. How do our attachments to others form the basis for knowledge? How do we come to know through and with others, in ways that are felt and valued as well as cognitively known? Carson McCullers's story, and the literary memoirs woven throughout this book, speak to these kinds of concerns more richly than many educational texts I now read. The value of literary texts for studying school learning practices therefore struck me as an important philosophical question. The feelings, histories, and attachments more overtly revealed in stories are things I have come to see as an important lens for shaping studies of learning.

That I would connect my evolving work to this particular group of philosophers is reflective of a lifelong passion for literary reading and writing. As a young girl growing up in a rural setting, I attached myself strongly to the children's storybooks we had around the house. I read stories printed in a set of Golden Books over and over, until these fictional texts became part of an imaginative world I created in a setting that otherwise wasn't all that "literary." The voices of people around me, the soothing rhythms of rural and small-town speech, also became part of a girlhood identity and imagination that were more complex than even culturally sensitive literacy research might suggest. As I later in life became involved in educational research, and specifically in research on language and literacy practices, I felt at times a sense of disappointment—like something was missing in the educational theory and research discourses that so formatively shaped my understandings. They seemed to miss important aspects of my childhood experiences in a certain historical, cultural, and class location, and my later readings of the childhood histories of Laurie and Jake. Literary texts seemed to capture what might be described as *complex particularity*—the histories, attachments, practices, and meanings that are best conveyed in a literary telling, a history. They also seemed to convey something else important for thinking about literacy learning—the agencies of students in response to language practices and values in their communities and classrooms. Strongly influenced by Bakhtin's essays on selfhood, agency, and narrative, I saw literary texts as a way of shaping a more nuanced story of working-class identities and school literacy learning.

My interests in literary shapings of educational research transformed the philosophical traditions on which I drew even as I embraced them. For instance, I came to value an underlying and little appreciated ethical stance that appears in Bakhtin's early philosophical essays. In Chapter 6, I describe how Bakhtin's commitments to seeing identity, understanding, relationship, and responsible action as connected threads have become commitments in my work as well. However, more so than Bakhtin, I came to see the writing of social science in literary ways, or in ways that allowed literary forms to mingle with social scientific ones, as itself a form of action in the world. I was strongly influenced by feminist writers such as Jane Miller and Valerie Walkerdine, who have allowed life histories, including their own, to inform their research and theorizing. The political activisms expressed in the work of these two theorists have become forms of action that I, too, wish to create in my writing. However, I also recognize that *fictions*, or literary shapings, have been of wider importance—extending beyond my life as an academic scholar, but also shaping that life. I have experimented with poetry and short fiction and immersed myself in literary stories and memoirs. I have been fascinated with life stories and literary tellings in ways that far exceed a theoretical "decision" to write as a feminist scholar. This is perhaps the same kind of passion that led the literary theorist Raymond Williams to read and write Marxist theory in novelistic ways and that led the novelist and philosopher Iris Murdoch to shape theory around an everyday story of relationship and love.

My passion for literary renderings of experience, my valuing of everyday creativity and imaginative response, and my commitment to more complex understandings of class-specific histories of learning—these are things I can no longer keep separate even as I seek to belong to communities of educational scholars. I engage with theory and research in essayist ways in this book, and I also allow a literary voice to surface and inform those more accepted practices of educational writing. I want to see the lives of Jake and Laurie in rich and complex ways, and to illuminate a different way of *seeing* everyday histories of language and learning in class settings. The histories of class and gender lived by these two children are just too complex for me to write in a different way.

The hybrid nature of this book allows it to be read by different readers in ways that reflect their varied commitments and interests in research and theory. Teachers who wish to think about practicing literacies with working-class children may find the chapters on Laurie and Jake (Chapters 4 and 5) especially engaging. In those chapters, I reflect on how painful stories of literacy engagements in school could have been different for these two children. My discussions of pedagogy, however, refuse to embrace a particular methodology as solution path, since I argue that this is not where activist teaching begins. For instance, some aspects of more progressive pedagogies (writing workshops, for example) were empowering for Jake and Laurie. However, these children also floundered within even the most well-intentioned progressive pedagogies, as their class identities bumped up against middle-class practices and expectations in school. In Chapters 4 and 5, I invite readers to join me in coming to know through intimate detail the values, attachments, and identities that Jake and Laurie experienced with family members at home, and then to juxtapose those experiences with school literacy practices.

In Chapters 2 and 6, I urge readers to consider those histories of class and gender location as starting points for reflection and critical action. In that sense, the theoretical or philosophical discussions in Chapters 2 and 6 are parts of an agenda for social activism and change in classrooms. Rather than argue for a method that will help fix things for working-class children, I urge teachers to read children's class, gender, and racially specific lives in ways that are more literary. From teachers' discerning readings of children's histories and language practices, I argue, emerge the teaching actions that draw on listening, watching, feeling, and understanding. This is how I view critical literacy practice.

In Chapter 3, I begin teasing apart the implications of allowing literary shapings of childhood experiences to mingle with the more typical discourses of educational research. I focus in that chapter on memories of working-class girlhoods. My emphasis in Chapter 3 on the early learning experiences of girls is in part a prelude to the following chapter, where I compose Laurie's history. This emphasis also reflects my concern that the interpretive lenses influencing my readings of young students' lives be evident. I insert details from my girlhood experiences into a multilayered analysis that considers how fictional shapings can inform literacy theory and research. In using the term *fictions*, I refer in Chapter 3 not to untruths (as in fact versus fiction) but, using Natalie Zemon Davis's (1987) phrasing, to "forming, shaping, and molding elements: the crafting of a narrative" (p. 3). The metaphor of *fictions* (e.g., fictions of girlhood, of boyhood, of literacy research) is a thread that surfaces in my narrative writing in Chapters 3–5, and in my final reflections on theory in Chapter 6.

Throughout this book is woven a critique of mainstream psychology and its hegemonic practices of description and analysis. Drawing on Valerie Walkerdine's work (e.g., 1984, 1998, 1990), I argue that educational theory and practice have been deeply informed by certain myths in the field of developmental psychology. To write in ways that are richly situated can help critique the developmental stories that are so importantly connected to educational politics and policies. That the writing of educational theory and research can help to change things is a powerful reason to risk taking on education and psychology as mutually shaping practices and ideologies. Perhaps my efforts to situate learning amid the smallness of lived histories can be a form of practice that cuts across boundaries of psychology, feminist theory, literacy research, and philosophy. It is the challenge of theory, argues Raymond Williams (1977), to help us move from the known to the unknown, searching for forms of expression that articulate our evolving commitments.

✣ 2 ✣

Situated Histories of Learning

Knowledge comes to form in human relationships. The world we notice
is the one that someone we cared about once pointed to.
>   —Madeleine Grumet, "The Language in the Middle"

A POWERFUL MYTH HAS SHAPED and sustained literacy research, in
spite of years of inquiry and classroom practice that run counter to its
underlying arguments. This is the myth that children approach literacy
practices as *autonomous reasoners* who then individually construct knowledge about literacy practices. Such myths not only miss a lot of the
complexity of how students engage with literacies. They also, through
their connections with certain philosophical traditions, divert the gazes
of teachers and researchers away from the particulars of coming to know
in historical and cultural localities, and amid relations with others. Stories
of autonomous learning have been influenced by philosophical traditions
aligned with certain rhetorical practices, namely, those associated with
(social) science and, especially, psychology. Michel Foucault (e.g., 1990)
writes of the discourses that shape institutions (such as schools), academic
disciplines (such as literacy research), and the subjects within them (such
as children, teachers, literacy researchers). The rhetorical practices that
have created and sustained literacy research are part of those disciplinary
shapings. Histories of particular localities and families, and of students'
individuated histories within them, can be readily lost in efforts to create
a generalized language of inquiry and practice. Feeling and valuing can
all too easily become divorced from knowing in social context, even within
research discourses that aim toward a more situated view of literacy
practices.

In this chapter, I engage responsively with the writings of two researchers and theorists whose work tackles head-on such myths as that of the autonomous reasoner and learner. In different ways and working in different disciplines, both theorists also address the relation of social class and gender to the what, why, and how of coming to *know* and *be* in cultural context. The theoretical perspectives of Shirley Brice Heath and Valerie Walkerdine could not be further apart in terms of disciplinary commitments and even forms of writing. And yet, I want to situate myself in a theoretical space between their work, as I aim toward creating a language of expression that best captures my own commitments. In subsequent chapters, I explore the merits of weaving narrative discourses into social science texts about literacy learning. I argue that philosophical metaphors are bound up with rhetorical practices and that altering our textual shapings of inquiry can have philosophical consequences. My use of narrative texts to write literacy research is part of an effort to situate individualism amid the richness and complexity of feeling, knowing, and valuing with others.

MYTHS OF AUTONOMY

There is good reason to believe that the myth of what feminist philosopher Genevieve Lloyd (1984) refers to as the Man of Reason permeates practices of literacy research. This is in part because literacy research and theory have been so closely aligned with the field of psychology. Viewed as a set of cognitive competencies, literacies are readily portrayed as objects "out there" in a symbolic world, waiting for learners to appropriate them in ways that prove independence and mastery. The idea that literacies are cultural and material *practices* shaped by histories, localities, and the persons within them that give form and meaning to children's lives has been resisted in part because of psychology's strong hold on educational theory and practice. Psychology's allegiance to science, with its metaphors of mastery and intellectual reasoning (Walkerdine, 1988), has created a politics of literacy education that distances our collective gaze from, as philosopher Lorraine Code (2000) argues, the specificity of "familial, social, cultural, or material location" (p. 219). Culturally and critically focused research has, however, challenged the notion that even something as "simple" as *naming* could exist outside of social, material, and affective relations with others. Rather, Code points out, as a child learns how to name, she also learns how to be, know, and feel in relation to others around her. Code quotes from bell hooks's (1996) memoir, *Bone Black*, in arguing for the cultural and affective specificity of even the most seemingly straightforward concepts, such as color terms:

We are so confused by this thing called Race.

We learn about color with crayons. We learn to tell the difference between white and pink and a color they call Flesh. The flesh-colored crayon
amuses us. . . . Flesh we know has no relationship to our skin, for we are
brown and brown and brown like all good things. (pp. 7–8)

Code argues that the field of developmental psychology has sustained
its metaphors of "solitary and detached individuals," and of reason's
preeminence over feeling, relationship, and cultural specificity, through
an alignment with powerful philosophical traditions (p. 217). Theory and
methods that have informed scientific practice also shape research on
learning. Prominent and influential literacy research texts (for instance,
Snow, Burns, & Griffin, 1998) argue that scientific inquiry provides the
most valid evidence about how students appropriate the skills and competencies associated with reading and writing. The field of literacy research,
often aligned with philosophical traditions that divorce reason from feeling, belonging, and acting with others, clings desperately to Enlighten-
ment Man even as cultural and critical literacy researchers aim to loosen
His stronghold on our inquiries. These powerful and particular (despite
claims to universality) practices of literacy research are readily appropriated within a conservative politics of education. A market-driven emphasis on individual achievement with its associated forms of practice
(e.g., proficiency testing, surveillance of teachers, normative labeling of
students) can be easily aligned with cognitive metaphors of autonomy
and mastery. However, a practice that locates itself on the "rough ground"
suggests alternatives to learners marching, like good soldiers, toward
independent mastery (Dunne, 1993). As Code (2000) writes:

Once inquiry locates itself "down on the ground," in the midst of and answerable to the integrity of real people's cognitive practices, it faces imperatives
that extend as far beyond the walls of the laboratory as beyond the walls of
the philosopher's study. These imperatives are about responsible inquiry;
about being "true to" the experiential situatedness of everyday knowings.
No longer can inquiry assume before-the-fact (= *a priori*) sameness of human
subjects either as inquirers or inquired into or before-the-fact (= *a priori*)
objective rational sameness on the part of inquirers themselves, whose inevi-
table situatedness cannot remain, epistemologically, *hors de question*. Nor can
inquiry mask its artefactual side, casting its object of inquiry—"the child"—in
a predetermined (*a priori* after all) image of a situationally indifferent, natu-
rally developing biological organism.

Most strange is the support these assumptions have provided for the
belief that people—subjects who are the objects of inquiry—can adequately
be known in this way, a belief that requires social scientists to restrict their

observations to separate, discrete behaviors and overt utterances of people extracted from the circumstances that generate those behaviors and make them possible, appropriate, and meaningful. They separate their subjects-objects of study out from their affective, cultural, racial, and economic circumstances; their bodily specificities as variously gendered, aged, abled beings; and the narratives that carry their psychosocial histories, constructing and constantly reconstructing the meanings that shape their lives. (pp. 235–236)

How difficult it has been, in spite of decades of culture-, class-, race-, and gender-sensitive inquiries, for the field of literacy research to shift its disciplinary lens to the specificity of which Code writes. If, however, even the most "simple" naming practice is saturated with the concreteness of place, history, and relationship, both social activism and inquiry would locate themselves amid those particulars. As Code suggests, responsible inquiry entails an effort to be "true to" the everyday practices of knowing. Divergent as they might be in terms of theoretical commitments, cultural and critical studies of learning both aim to produce such situated accounts. Let me illustrate these two perspectives by reflecting on a moment in the family life of Jake, one of the two children whom I came to know across 3 years of research.

It is a warm spring day in April, and Jake is feeling his oats. He is outside playing with Lee Ann, his young sister (she is 4), and two older cousins—a teenage boy and a girl who is about 10 or 11 years old. Jake's mom, his mom-mom (maternal grandmother), and I are sitting in front of the house watching the kids play. Large empty boxes are strewn around the front yard (from his father's mechanical contracting business?), and Jake and his cousins have decided how they are going to use them. Jake gets inside one of the boxes, and his teenage cousin picks up the box and starts swirling Jake around. Lee Ann gets a turn, too; her cousin more carefully swings her around inside the box, with the adult women sitting in front of the porch voicing their caution to "be careful!" The energy level is high; the kids seem charged with the spring air and thrill of being swung around. However, things turn sour as Lee Ann and Jake get into a tiff. It starts with Jake calling Lee Ann a "chicken" when she complains about a small scrape on her elbow. With the encouragement of her mom-mom and mom, Lee Ann retorts in a singsong fashion:

LEE ANN: Jake is a chicken!
          Jake is a chicken!
          Jake is a chicken!
          Jake is a chicken!

Jake gets out of cardboard box and gives Lee Ann a hard shove. Lee Ann falls to the ground, crying.

As someone now identifying with middle-class values and language practices, I expect to see Jake's mom and mom-mom "educate" him. The responses from Jake's mom, mom-mom, and older cousins, however, are more direct and to the point:

MOM: JAKE!
        You don't push her down!
        [*to Lee Ann*] Don't take that from him!

Lee Ann comes crying to adult women.

BOY COUSIN: Kick him in his butt!
Jake crawls back inside cardboard box
MOM-MOM: You go take care of him, Lee
MOM: You go take care of him
DEBORAH: He's helpless right now, Lee!
MOM: Oh yeah
        Go jump on him!
BOY COUSIN: Jump on him [*Holds down box with Jake inside*]
        Jump on him!
        Hurry!
Jake has started to roll (inside the box) toward the sidewalk, but an older girl cousin leads Lee Ann to the box and holds it down by its corners. She helps Lee Ann get on the box and start to bounce on top of it, with Jake still inside. Jake lets out some high-pitched, fake-sounding screams.

MOM-MOM: Lee, jump on him!
DEBORAH: She's getting her revenge now!
MOM: She's getting her revenge, Jake!
JAKE: Let me out!
        High-pitched screams
        Let me out!
        Let me out!

This episode from Jake's home life in second grade is hardly a moment of literacy learning. No written texts are involved; nothing literary is evoked in these lived moments. Nonetheless, both cultural and critical literacy researchers would argue that such moments of living have a lot to do with how children later engage with school literacies. However, the *ways* in which such theories depict relations between children's histories of learning and their literate engagements in school differ in emphasis and argument. As Cleo Cherryholmes (1993) might argue, culturally and critically focused theorists tell different stories about literacy learning in situated contexts. Though both cultural and critical researchers work to dispel myths of autonomous individualism, they do so in ways that differ philosophically and rhetorically.

Cultural literacy researchers might tell their readers about processes of socialization that involve language practices, ways of acting, values, and beliefs. The *ways with words* (Heath, 1983) voiced by Jake, Lee Ann, and their mom and mom-mom reflect the working-class practices and values of the community in which they lived. Jake and Lee Ann's mom-mom lived right up the road from their home; the cultural continuity of practices and values shared among generations was stable and consistent. Physically (after all, Lee Ann was led by the arm and physically shown how to get her revenge!) and through particular forms of expression, Jake and Lee Ann were being socialized into ways of being, knowing, talking, acting, and feeling. Cultural literacy researchers would argue that these culturally specific ways with words, or what James Paul Gee (1996) refers to as *Discourses*, are related in important ways to how children engage with school literacies. It is not just children's preschool engagements with written texts per se that make such a difference once they enter school, nor even their engagements with stories and other types of oral literacies. Rather, it is an entire cultural web—a cat's cradle, if you will—of language practices and identities that so importantly has an impact on school learning, including literacy learning. Thus, young Jake and Lee Ann were—in moments like these—becoming and knowing within practices involving language and action. For cultural literacy researchers, the fact that some of these *knowings* and *becomings* might not mesh with school literacy practices is central to their theorizing, research, and social activism.

Alternatively, those who draw their metaphors and forms of inquiry from the related fields of critical psychology, critical discourse analysis, and feminist theory and practice might write in ways that convey the shifting relations of power, gender, and class played out in this moment of living. This episode in Jake's life could be read as centrally about both power and gender. Jake throws around his weight, and Lee Ann is subjectively positioned in ways that empower her as well. Identities reflective of gender are interwoven in moments of living. Lee Ann is wearing a dress, shoes with a strap, and white socks. Jake is in jeans and a T-shirt. Lee Ann is swirled cautiously compared to Jake, perhaps reflecting her younger age as well as gender. She comes running to the adult women when shoved by her brother. For critical literacy researchers and psychologists, these discourses being voiced by adults and enacted by the children create shifting *locations* in which Jake and Lee Ann practice identities and forms of knowing. As the children participate in discourses that reflect class-specific ways of being a girl or boy, the discourses that they live become aspects of who they are and what they desire. Social discourses achieve their power as they construct children as thinking, feeling, and desiring subjects within them. Jake can voice and enact a macho discourse, for instance, by giving Lee Ann a shove when she positions him as a "chicken." A university researcher can locate herself as a reader of this moment of living by thinking of ways Jake might act and think more sensitively. His mom and mom-mom can voice their values and identities by telling Lee Ann, "You go take care of him."

For critical psychologists and critical literacy researchers, none of these discursive locations and associated power relations are fixed or unchanging. Nor are they the "property" of individuals or even the communities in which individuals live and learn. Rather, they are shifting relations *between* discourses, taken up in ways reflecting the histories and cultural locations of those who practice them. Those histories are portrayed in ways that complicate, or *refract*, the identities that cultural researchers sometimes depict more univocally. In school, children can gain or lose power and associated kinds of knowledge as they take up social discourses. They can act, talk, and know in *hybrid* ways as well. Individualism, for those who write critically about discourses and subjectivities, is a site for considerable conflict but also for activism and change. If children's identities are not fixed but provisional, classroom practices can help create new subject positions. Children can know and be in ways that transgress racist, classist, and sexist oppressions—a key goal of critical literacy education. Children and teachers together can contest and transform the relations that position children as "failures" because they voice and enact working-class identities and values, or Black identities and values. Critical literacy educators work to use situated inquiries as a platform from which to study and transform social injustices. Poststructuralist theories of language and selfhood are lenses for analysis as well as critical action.

How these two lenses on learning in social context have shaped my own work is the topic to which I now turn. As I locate myself between them, I will spend time with the work of the two foundational theorists who have been especially influential for me. The writings of Valerie Walkerdine and Shirley Brice Heath are, I argue, important lenses for unpacking the philosophical underpinnings of the autonomous individuals that cultural literacy researchers have sought to locate in cultural time and space, and that critical literacy researchers have sought to liberate from the shackles of racist, classist, and sexist oppression.

However, I won't stop with those readings. For there is something that, for me as a reader of cultural and critical literacy research, remains oblique. It is the value and meaning of a touch, the look in one's eye, a shared moment of living in which an imaginative space is opened up for both teacher and student, or caretaker and child. These moments of living engender the memories, imaginings, and histories experienced with others who have meaning in our lives. That such particulars become distanced from theoretical dialogues about learning is a reflection, in part, of impoverished theories of discourse and, as a consequence, impoverished theories of learning. This is a loss to educational researchers both philosophically (it doesn't make sense) and ethically (it engenders practice divorced from lived realities). For as Code has suggested, there is no moment of learning, even "simple" naming, that occurs outside of relations infused with feeling and value, and formed through attachments with others.

CULTURAL AND CRITICAL RESEARCH ON LEARNING: TWO READINGS

Working from the perspective of an anthropologist and a literacy educator, Shirley Brice Heath spent a decade immersing herself in the language practices and community lives of children and adults living in two working-class communities in the Piedmont. As Heath (1983) describes the purposes of that work, her research lens was focused on creating ethnographies of communication—richly descriptive texts that chronicled the "face-to-face network in which each child learns the ways of acting, believing, and valuing of those about him" (p. 6). Her perspective on language, strongly influenced by the grounding of this study in cultural anthropology, can be aligned with Wittgenstein's use of the phrase *forms of life* (1980). Rather than viewing language practices solely as linguistic texts, Heath focused on the histories and social ecologies of *language practices*. As she writes, "The ways of living, eating, sleeping, worshiping, using space, and filling time which surrounded these language learners would have to be accounted for as part of the milieu in which the processes of language learning took place" (1983, p. 3).

Important to Heath's work was the spatial and temporal location of the research amid life in *these* two communities. Her narrative descriptions and general commentaries often remind the reader of the situated nature of the research and the importance of location for the generalizations that emerged. What could more superficially be derived as generalized themes regarding working-class language practices and identities were presented in her text as identities of *place*, reflective of the particulars of life in two specific cultural settings. Heath discussed identity distinctions such as race, class, and gender, but from the point of view of the practices unique to these communities. The historicity of this piece of research and its grounding in relationships constructed over time was part of what enabled Heath to know in intimate detail the forms of life practiced in Roadville and Trackton. What emerged was a text that integrated social histories of place with fine-grained ethnographies of community language practices.

In my reading of *Ways with Words*, I want to focus on three themes. First, I consider the ways in which children's *knowings* are presented in Heath's study as saturated with the cultural specificities of time/space locations, family and community relationships, and values—all filtered through shared language practices. Second, I want to reflect on how this study describes relations of gender and class in racially distinctive communities. Finally, I turn to how literacy practices are portrayed in Heath's text. A close reading of *Ways with Words*, I argue, disrupts the myth that children come to know the worlds and words of their homes, communities, and classrooms through autonomous mastery. Rather, child learners come to *be* and *know* with others as they engage in discourse practices fully saturated with cultural meanings.

Children's learning is depicted in *Ways with Words* as layered within culturally specific uses of time, space, and objects. Children in Roadville learn the proper use of time and space—such as neatly arranged objects in one's room (p. 116) and specific routines for eating, playing, and sleeping (p. 145). Children in Trackton experience time and space within the complex social textures of child rearing shared among extended family and community members. Carried from one interactional setting to another, Trackton babies are immersed in the fluidity of shifting forms of talk and social relations. As Heath writes, "time and space have few restraints [in Trackton]; their only limits are interactional" (p. 146). Amid these situated practices, knowing how to feel and act is part of language and reasoning. Young learners in Trackton, for instance, must know when and how to respond quickly to changes in mood as they participate in multiple-party interactions (p. 82). Young Roadville children learn to act and feel in ways that respect the rightness of the biblical Word (p. 138).

Heath writes of how girls and boys are socialized within gendered practices in Trackton and Roadville. Objects construct different cultural worlds for boys and girls; language practices create different ways of being and knowing with others. Masculine and feminine identities play out in these two working-class settings in ways reflective of racial differences refracted through histories and geographies. Boy children in Trackton, for instance, become storytellers in multiparty interactions on front porches. They perform stories in ways that are gendered and that draw on oral traditions of Black communities. Story performances are connected to practices that shape different social worlds for girls and boys. Heath recounts, for instance, how girls and older siblings wait patiently as wage earners on Friday afternoon distribute treats first to young boy children (p. 71). Roadville children also grow up within gendered social worlds. Consonant with the value placed upon "rightness" in Roadville, the object worlds that surround girls and boys are sharply demarcated. Girls play with Raggedy Ann dolls and dollhouses; boys, with plastic soldiers and toy trucks (p. 133).

In *Ways with Words*, language practices are depicted as aspects of the social histories and cultural forms of life that fully saturate cognitive concepts. Infused with feeling, value, and the specificity of place, oral and literate language activities—storytelling, talking junk, gossip, telling it right, reading and writing letters—are described as practices lived out within differing cultural and class localities. In a summary of traditions of storytelling, for instance, Heath points out the connections between the valuing of rightness among Roadville community members and oral stories heard and later voiced by young speakers:

> In Roadville, children come to know a story as either a retold account from a book, or a factual account of a real event in which some type of marked behavior occurred, and there is a lesson to be learned. There are Bible stories, testimonials, sermons, and accounts of hunting, fishing, cooking, working, or other daily events. Any fictionalized account of a real event is viewed as a lie; reality is better than fiction. Roadville's church and community life admit no story other than that which meets the definition internal to the group. (p. 187)

These culturally saturated language and literacy practices, Heath argues, are central to educational research and advocacy. As children enter classrooms, they encounter worlds that are also saturated with specific cultural meanings, values, and forms of knowing. Conflict occurs, however, when the ways with words of communities and classrooms differ to the point that school language practices are unfamiliar, foreign, to children living on the margins of middle-class institutional structures. Heath found that Roadville children, for instance, engaged readily with the "rightness" of learning their ABCs. However, their participation in the discourses of school became more fragile when asked to imagine or hypothesize in ways that depart from the trueness of printed words or factual experience.

For Roadville children, their community's ways of learning and talking about what one knows both parallel and contradict the school's approach to stories. In the classroom, occasions for storytelling between adults and children are established by adult request, just as they are in Roadville at home. Teachers sometimes politely listen to very young children's spontaneous stories (for example, those volunteered during a reading lesson), but these are not valued as highly as those specifically requested by adults as part of a preplanned lesson. Unsolicited stories are often seen as digressions. When teachers ask children to "make up" a story from their reading book, they prefer fanciful, creative, and imaginative accounts. In Roadville, such stories told by children would bring punishment or a charge of lying. The summary of one story can be linked with another, but extension of the facts of a story by hyperbole without qualification, and the transfer of characters, times, and places would be unacceptable features of stories in Roadville. (p. 296)

Part of the importance of Heath's work is that she didn't stop at cultural description, no matter how richly composed it might be. Her empirical research was combined with advocacy, as she worked collaboratively with teachers to create more culturally responsive pedagogies. Working alongside teacher ethnographers in her university courses, she helped their young students juxtapose community language practices with school literacies, as students learned to articulate language differences and move *between* cultural worlds. Heath helped teachers to construct more permeable (Dyson, 1993) or culturally hybrid (Gutiérrez, Baquedano-López, Alvarez, & Chiu, 1999) classroom spaces where students could begin to move between cultural discourses without giving up the richness of their community experiences and language practices. With its forms of activism rooted in the close study of cultural specifics, this research project was more liberatory than many projects that refer to themselves by the phrase "critical literacy." More oblique in this research and advocacy project, however, was a political awareness that would allow us to see those culturally infused language practices through an ideological lens. The politics of educational change is, however, part of the social history that Heath writes. For the changes that occurred in one historical moment, she tells us in a concluding chapter, became fragile amid the tightening of curriculum mandates that occurred in the 1980s.

A politically attuned lens, however, might have other stories to tell about the cultural ways with words of which Heath so eloquently writes. For how did the young working-class children in two community localities learn to know, feel, talk, read, and write in relation to injustices they were sure to experience growing up in the rural Southeast? As readers, we reflect on the cultural regularities of community life and wonder perhaps about the feelings, knowings, and belongings of subjects within those discourses. What Valerie Walkerdine and Helen Lucey (1989) describe as a *politics of subjectivity* focuses our gaze more directly on subjectivities lived out amid relations of power. Somewhere, in the midst of these social histories, children learned to confront the pain of class difference—the otherness they must have experienced as they engaged with school discourses. Somewhere, too, teachers had to confront their own racisms and classisms before they could see the richness of children's culturally saturated lives. Our eyes are diverted from these politics of education and politics of subjectivity, even as we come to know through ethnographic description the particulars of words, values, and education in two communities. Still, the detailed studies of culturally infused ways with words strongly contest any illusions we might have about children's "independent mastery" of literate discourses. Words, time, space, objects—all come to the child learner enveloped in culturally specific practices and are brought to awareness by caretakers who are the primary others in the child's early life.

Working within a political context in which *class* is much more salient than in the United States, Valerie Walkerdine articulates an explicitly class- and gender-specific position. She situates her critical and feminist readings of psychology and education within the history of her own working-class childhood and within a feminist politics. Part of her project aims to unveil how children are positioned as subjects within discourses, including the discourses of mainstream developmental psychology, which, Walkerdine argues, are "coupled" with mainstream education. She deconstructs traditional (i.e., middle-class, patriarchal) readings of "the child" and children's development as she seeks to construct alternate readings. As Walkerdine (1988) writes at the conclusion of her critical reading of developmental psychology, *The Mastery of Reason*, "In many places psychologists are struggling to tell other stories—stories of women, of blacks—stories of marginality which refuse to celebrate *the* child but will no longer be silent" (p. 216; emphasis added).

Walkerdine's critical studies take her into social locations ranging from the kitchen to the classroom, varied sites in which, as she argues, children's subjectivities are produced within discourses reflective of relations such as gender, race, and class. For instance, in their analyses of child language transcripts from a study of language at home and school (Tizard & Hughes, 1985), Walkerdine and Lucey (1989) argue for a class-sensitive reading of transcripts that depict mothers' interactions with their 4-year-old daughters at home. Critical of readings that portray middle-class mothers as "sensitive" to the educational needs of their young daughters in contrast with working-class mothers' more linguistically "restricted" engagements, Walkerdine and Lucey question the frameworks that construct particular truths about mothering practices, child development, and education. Their work expresses a political commitment to unpacking the "regimes of truth" (Foucault, 1990) that have led to the naturalization of certain practices and the pathologization of others. They write:

> Our aim here in exploring these examples [of mother/daughter language transcripts] is not so much to criticize Tizard and Hughes as to understand why certain views of development, which are common to most modern developmental psychology, make the assumptions that they do and the effect this has when used as an interpretive framework on data about development and therefore also about mothering. We end up with a framework which is unable to link what a particular four-year-old does or does not know to any theory which takes into account the social, material, and economic specificity of the lives of the children concerned. (Walkerdine & Lucey, 1989, p. 93)

Their alternative readings are focused on how mothers and daughters are produced or *regulated* as subjects within discourses reflective of material and economic relations. Mothering as a set of practices is situated in race, class, and gender relations, which in turn are linked to a politics of education and psychology. Mothering practices, for instance, are read within a politics of a liberal democracy, in which children ideally become free, reasoning agents. Sensitive mothers are those who produce such children—the verbally articulate reasoner within the National Council of Teachers of Mathematics (NCTM) standards; the creative young author within whole-language pedagogies.

Part of the richness of Walkerdine's work is that her class- and gender-sensitive readings of psychology and education are interwoven with her own history of growing up in the working classes in postwar Britain. Her life story becomes part of her political action as she reads psychological theory and language data through the lens of her childhood history and the histories of other working class women. Walkerdine and Lucey, for instance, write of the anger they felt as they read language transcripts of working-class mothers and daughters at home and then confronted other researchers' interpretive readings of those transcripts. The *difference* ascribed to working-class language practices hit them as a research problematic. "Why," they asked, "was *this* afternoon chosen for discussion, which seemed to both of us so very like many afternoons we had spent with our mothers, completely recognisable and unremarkable?" (p. 7; emphasis in original). As they later began to unpack what they describe as fictions of "natural" mothering, they drew on their class histories as locations from which to construct feminist and class-sensitive readings. The theorizing that emerged was a form of engaged politics rooted as much in class histories as in poststructuralist theories of discourse. The politics of subjectivity that is threaded throughout Walkerdine's work reflects a politically infused act of reading her working-class girlhood, developmental theory, and education through a lens that does not discount the specificity of class (Walkerdine & Lucey, 1989), and class-specific femininities (Walkerdine, 1990).

In *The Mastery of Reason*, Walkerdine (1988) looks at mathematical terms as one instance of how meanings are part of social relations that are realized in discourses. Her aim in exploring children's mathematical understandings is to unpack a topic of inquiry—children's mathematics development—that has long aligned itself with scientific objectivism. Taking on Piaget's arguments that the developing child constructs an understanding of mathematical universals such as relational terms (e.g., big, little), Walkerdine argues instead that mathematical reasonings are practices within discourses. She uses the example of a classroom discussion of relational terms. When asked to name which of three bears (Daddy Bear, Mummy Bear, Baby Bear) was biggest, preschool children insisted that Mummy Bear was the biggest, though Daddy Bear was perceptually larger. Within a set of *family* relations, however, Mummy Bear could indeed be "bigger," Walkerdine argues (p. 46). Daddy Bear might be less emotionally salient, or he might be physically nonpresent (see Code, 2000). Physical or mathematical terms, like all meanings, are produced within practices (see Walkerdine & Lucey, 1989).

> If a word does not simply represent physical relation, but rather provides the basis whereby any particular physical relation is inscribed as a relation within the organization of a practice, then we are not justified in speaking simply of "representation". If children only learn such relations through their own insertion into a relational dynamic within such practices, we can argue that they become a subject as, and in, those relations. Such relations are multiple. How far, then, is this the same as talking of the acquisition of concepts or of meanings as though it were a function of an object world, a physical world, a physical environment, or a structure or process *applied* to the social world. Previously, I have used the term "always-already social" (Henriques *et al*, 1984) to imply that there is no physical relation for any infant which is not always and already a social relation. (Walkerdine, 1988, pp. 15–16; emphasis in the original)

Children's agencies and understandings are shifted in this critique to the discourses that regulate them as knowing subjects. Meanings do not adhere in knowing subjects, but rather subjects are constructed as they take up positions within discourse practices. Linking this poststructuralist account of how children come to know within cultural, material, and economic locations to a politics of subjectivity, Walkerdine and Lucey (1989) ask how discourses become part of children's lived realities, including psychic realities. Pain, fantasy, material and economic conditions—all are part of practices that involve power and that create various locations for children to *know* and to *be*. As Walkerdine and Lucey write, "What we require is an analysis of how regulation is 'lived'"(p. 35).

Meanings and subjectivities are lived, Walkerdine argues, within discourses that entail shifting relations of power. Children take up different power positions and forms of knowledge in their engagements *through* discourses. In the transcript below from *Schoolgirl Fictions* (Walkerdine, 1990), two preschool boys achieve a position of power by taking up a patriarchal and sexualized discourse that regulates their female teacher accordingly. The moment of positioning in discourses begins when a classmate, Annie, takes a Lego piece from the area where the two boys, Sean and Terry, are working:

Terry tries to take it [the Lego piece] away from [Annie] to use himself, and she resists. He says:

Terry: You're a stupid cunt, Annie.

The teacher tells him to stop and Sean tries to mess up another child's construction. The teacher tells him to stop. Then Sean says:

Sean: Get out of it Miss Baxter paxter.
Terry: Get out of it knickers Miss Baxter.
Sean: Get out of it Miss Baxter paxter.
Terry: Get out of it Miss Baxter the knickers paxter knickers, bum.
Sean: Knickers, shit, bum.
Miss B: Sean, that's enough, you're being silly.
Sean: Miss Baxter, knickers, show your knickers.
Terry: Miss Baxter, show your bum off. (*they giggle*)
Miss B: I think you're being very silly.
Terry: Shit Miss Baxter, shit Miss Baxter.
Sean: Miss Baxter, show your knickers your bum off.
Sean: Take all your clothes off, your bra off.
Terry: Yeah, and take your bum off, take your wee-wee off, take your
          clothes, your mouth off.
Sean: Take your teeth out, take your head off, take your hair off, take
          your bum off. Miss Baxter the paxter knickers taxter.
Miss B: Sean, go and find something else to do please. (p. 4)

Power, Walkerdine argues, is produced within discourses, as are the subjects who are variously regulated by their shifting positionings within discourses. Preschoolers Terry and Sean in the above example can locate their adult female teacher in a discourse of male sexuality and power. Practices create subjectivities as children and teachers take them up and become knowing and feeling subjects within them.

This does not mean that these socially produced knowings and feelings are any less a part of learners' individuated realities. Walkerdine (1990) argues that what in more psychoanalytic literatures might be referred to as our psyches, including unconscious psychic realities, are produced in discourses. Texual shapings of an always-already social world—media images, stories, film, comic books, talk—create fictions that become realities for individuated subjects. For instance, textual or media images, and educational spaces that inscribe girls as subjects within them, become lived and felt realities. Fantasies, Walkerdine argues, are no less powerful than material realities. Girlhood is textually produced in fictions that are read back as fact, becoming part of girls' individuated subjectivities as they become inscribed in pedagogical discourses *about* girls. Painful contradictions and suppressions can occur as educational discourses create certain textual spaces for girls, ones that often leave out sexualities and passions amid their "impossible fictions" of knowing as intellectual mastery (p. 120). Girls can be located within contradictory subject positions: passive caretaker versus active learner, "good girl" versus desiring subject (p. 119). Drawing on psychoanalytic literatures, Walkerdine writes of the splitting that can occur as girls live out these contradictions:

> The denial [of fictions] in the pedagogic discourses and practices, and the wider cultural denial of which they are a part, is lived out by these little girls in the way they are positioned and see themselves as good, poor, and bad, and the splitting and denial which this engenders.
>
> Uncovering the fictions of our formation is about examining our inscription within those fantasies. In that sense "woman" and "child" in all their guises are impossible fictions, yet fictions invested so powerfully in the practices which make up the veridicality of the present social order. (p. 124)

Children's subjectivities are never unitary. As Walkerdine (1990) writes, "the constitution of subjectivity is not all of one piece, without seams and ruptures" (p. 30). However, these "seams and ruptures," at times a source of painful conflict, also entail the possibility of change. Changes in pedagogical practices and the subjects they produce require, first, unpacking the fictions that shape children (and teachers) within normative lenses. An explicitly political activism is required if the dis-

courses that create "knowers" and "knowings" are to be altered. Walkerdine sets her feminist readings of psychology and education within a
political action frame that aims to reveal other stories, other readings.
This is a hopeful critique for educators. For teachers, too, might long to
tell "other stories" of their marginalities, and those of their students, amid
powerful and patriarchal discourses of schooling, testing, and surveillance. Unlike Heath's account of the critical action that ensued from her
studies of ways with words, Walkerdine's work does not explicitly engage
with educational activism. We can read her feminist critique, however,
as a form of political action, since she frames her theoretical purposes as
such. Her work becomes a lens through which to "read" children's identities and situated knowings differently. It becomes more difficult to divert
our gaze from the educational stories that marginalize working-class children, Blacks, girls, women teachers—having engaged responsively with
her critical readings and rewritings. Creating new possibilities for subjectivities and forms of knowledge is part of a critical project aimed at
deconstructing and changing social relations.

Walkerdine's critical readings of education and psychology can
be aligned with new dialogues about literacy education. *Critical literacy*
has become an umbrella term for politically sensitive research and practice
that aims to change social injustices. Such work draws on frameworks
similar to those informing Walkerdine's writing—poststructuralist
theories of discourse, critical discourse analysis, and feminism (see
McLaren & Lankshear, 1993). Critical literacy educators strive to unpack
and ultimately change social injustices that hinge on inequitable power
relations. Often drawing on the writings of Brazilian educator Paulo
Freire (e.g., 1999), critical literacy theorists argue for reading and writing
as sites of social praxis (reflection and action). Readings of texts, they
argue, are always politically infused. Critical literacy educators can work
with students to bring to awareness the silencings and oppressions that
can be embedded in texts and their readings. As Barbara Comber
(1998) writes, the literacy classroom can be a nexus for social critique and
action:

> When teachers and students are engaged in critical literacy they will be
> asking complicated questions about language and power, about people and
> lifestyle, about morality and ethics, about who is advantaged by the ways
> things are and who is disadvantaged. On the basis of their analysis they'll
> also be taking action to make a positive difference. Critical literacy resists
> any simplistic or generic definitions because the agenda is to understand the
> complexity of the relationships between language practices, power relations,
> and identities.

Critical literacy occurs when teachers work with students to understand and contest the ways in which language contributes to injustice and when students and teachers use language and literacy to learn about and change injustice. It requires conversations between teachers and students about the ways in which texts work to maintain and promote the unequal distribution of wealth, information, status, property, influence, and power. It requires teachers to become text analysts and to know what is involved in writing for social change. To work towards a socially critical literacy is not unproblematic. It requires that we look at the ways we read the world; it requires examining what we take for granted, what texts tell us about the way things are and why they are the way they are. (p. 9).

Critical literacy educators and researchers often write of enabling children to see and, at times, rewrite the identities that are shaped for them by school and school texts. Bronwyn Davies (1993), for instance, writes about helping young readers to deconstruct their readings of texts and the ways in which texts "write" them as subjects. As she says about her work with even very young readers and writers:

Instead of being informed by an authoritative text, or of deciding whether or not they like a text, or whether or not the text is "realistic" . . . critical/deconstructive writing, as I am conceptualizing it here, enables children to see the text as shaping them and shaping worlds in ways that have previously been invisible to them. . . . It involves finding a way to make the shaping process visible, to "catch the text in the act" of shaping. (pp. 62–63)

Critical literacy education can be a means of helping students to become aware of the fictions (as Walkerdine would argue) that shape them as readers, writers, and acting subjects. This movement has become a nexus of arguments for a more empowering form of literacy education, particularly for children living on the margins of middle-class power structures (see Finn, 1999). However, something can be lost in moving from the work of class- and gender-sensitive theorists such as Walkerdine into forms of educational activism. Walkerdine's critique was built on a politics focused on how power is *lived* by subjects amid the locations of class, gender, race, economics, and history. Too often, critical theorists in education aim for social analysis and critique, but from a vantage point that is more distant from those material, lived realities. The specificities of history, locality, and class can sometimes be oddly missing from educational discourses that strive toward getting students to read and write critically. We see students engaged in critical readings—but know little of their subjectivities, nor those of their teacher. The affective relations among students and teachers in relation to texts fall out of focus. And yet, aren't those relations, those histories that emerge in class locations, part of the "always-already social" of which Walkerdine writes?

"We have small lives, easily lost in foreign droughts or famines," writes A. L. Kennedy (1990) in her collection of short stories, *Night Geometry and the Garscadden Trains*. There is something of the smallness of our childhood histories, the concreteness of living and knowing with others in class-specific localities, that can easily be lost in efforts to practice and research emancipatory literacy education. However, the smallness of how power is lived by women, girls, Blacks, and working-class people may be crucial to the feminist activism for which Walkerdine argues theoretically.

As I attempt to situate myself in a critical space between her writings and those of cultural researchers such as Heath, I find myself drawn to intimate histories, to stories of class and gender locations. I view Walkerdine's work as an important vantage point for theorizing how children learn to be and know in class and gender locations. Her explicitly political focus on the "always-already social" of children's subjectivities creates a theoretical language for talking about how practices are lived amid relations of power. The refracted images of her own working-class girlhood become part of a feminist politics that situates "the child" in economic, material, and discursive space. Sexuality, materiality, fantasy—all are part of a (re)reading and (re)writing of developmental psychology and education, and the child subjects they shape.

It is the smallness of situated lives, however, that I ultimately find the most significant for both theorizing and activism. Culturally infused practices, lived in sometimes painful power relations, achieve their meaning and weight because of their connection with particular others in children's lives. The discourses that socialize and regulate children as knowing, feeling subjects are replete with the sociality of race, class, and gender locations. And yet these discourses are voiced by others in ways that "shade" or intone them responsively. Children's engagements in discourse practices are responsive as well—imaginative, resistant, ironic, sad, curious. Perhaps most importantly, as children and their caretakers (or teachers) engage in discourse practices, they create shared histories of response that become part of contexts of meaning. Maybe these small histories can begin to tell other stories about how practices shape individuated subjectivities.

The smallness of lived histories could be a starting place, I will argue, for inquiries that strive to be true to the particulars of children's situated lives. Literary discourses can be a useful means of coming to know in the ways that I describe. Narrative discourses focus our gaze on complex particularity; they portray *knowing* and *knowers* in historicized and situated ways. As I search for a critical space for inquiry, I engage with both literary discourses and philosophical ones. Childhood histories and theoretical essays about narrative, selfhood, and knowledge become part of those hybrid efforts. I begin with a story from my childhood, one that takes me back to the particulars of a rural southeastern town, vacation Bible school, and Jesus.

✦ 3 ✦

Memories of Working-Class Girlhoods

A reader is a person in history, a person with a history.
—Jane Miller, *Seductions*

WHEN I WAS A YOUNG GIRL, I used to spend part of my summers coloring pictures of Jesus. I spent the early parts of my childhood in rural North Carolina, in an Appalachian town nestled in the "hills," as the locals would say. This was part of the Bible Belt Southeast, God's country. If ever for a moment driving down the road you should forget the Word, there it would appear, posted on a sign along the side of the road: JESUS IS COMING. In the summers, I attended vacation Bible school, two weeks of having warm interactions with churchgoing women, playing with other children, and being socialized as a young southern girl. There, I would dutifully color pictures of Jesus as I sipped on Kool Aid and munched on cookies. And our vacation Bible school class would sing songs: "Jesus loves me, yes I know / For the Bible tells me so." Talk about processes of regulation and culturally specific socialization! There I was, learning to be a "good girl" as I sang, colored, and more generally practiced the fundamentalist discourses of the rural Southeast. And yet my memories of those practices defy the theories that depict them as processes of social-ization and regulation. Sure, they were powerful discourses. After all, there was the visceral threat of rotting in Hell. Still, I didn't approach them or take them up as literal truths, but rather as imaginative spaces for response and transformation. The visual arts of coloring, stories I had heard about Him, and stories from my own experience were juxtaposed in moments of transforming pictures of Jesus into colorful displays. Looking back, I can see those poetic moments as the beginnings of literary experi-ence, ones that forecast the life of a young reader.

Such are the histories of knowing and knowers. We never engage in cultural practices as sponges, simply appropriating cultural meanings or being positioned within power relations. Rather, learning also entails small, and at times imperceptible, moments of shading, valuing, and imaginative reconstruction. Those small moments and histories are as critical to a theory of learning as what we might describe as socialization or positioning in discourses. Very importantly, practices occur in engagement with others, such as the caretakers who help shape learners' values, feelings, and attachments at a young age.

For instance, in my history of growing up surrounded by Christian discourses, I remember an ironic look in my mother's eyes as she threatened me with the consequences of not being good (everyone understanding, of course, the truth that not being "good" could lead one down the wrong path, in a downward spiral to the place where sinners go). The fundamentalist discourses of the rural Southeast were infused with an ironic twist, similar to the ways adults might talk to children about Santa Claus. My relations with particular others in my girlhood, those pointing to a world before I had a chance to know it, created the conditions for my quite literary readings of Jesus and His Word. Those readings were part of an imaginative space made possible through the particulars of knowing and feeling in relation with others. My teachers in vacation Bible school were formative others, too, but their gaze, their touch, did not have the special meaning of someone whose connection with me involved a loving value context.

In "The Generalized and Concrete Other," the philosopher Seyla Benhabib (1992) writes in similar ways about subjects' identities. Rather than depicting identities in terms of generalized relations that regulate, socialize, or position, she portrays them as aspects of a life history or narrative. We are situated and shaped within the particulars of that narrative, Benhabib argues. In that sense, the socializing and regulative processes about which cultural and critical theorists write are threads of subjects' histories. And yet children are agents within those histories, agents *of* them as well. Moreover, the others who first point to the cultural and affective worlds that children come to know are concrete others. The situated individual of whom Benhabib (1992) writes is an embodied individual who feels, knows, and imagines with others as she intones her experiences in ways that become part of a unique life story:

> Identity does not refer to my potential for choice alone, but to the actuality of my choices, namely to how I, as a finite, concrete, embodied individual, shape and fashion the circumstances of my birth and family, linguistic, cultural and gender identity into a coherent narrative that stands as my life

story. Indeed if we recall that every autonomous being is one born of others and not, as Rawls, following Hobbes, assumes, a being "not bound by prior moral ties to another," the question becomes: how does this finite, embodied creature constitute into a coherent narrative those episodes of choice and limitation, agency and suffering, initiative and dependence? (pp. 161–162)

Jane Miller similarly writes of children's identities emerging in their earliest relationships, often with mothers as important dialogic others. Recalling Lorraine Code's comments about naming, Miller (1990) argues that gender is shaped in relation to the specificities of those early words and attachments:

It is surely within those first conversations, those shared sightings and namings, that the specificity, the material detail and concrete knowing of the world are learned as values within an actual, evolving culture. The development from this first learning to children's . . . movement away from mothers, away from home, will vary vitally according to class, place, time. Gender is always learned, however, and by children of both sexes, through these earliest articulations and manifestations of difference and similarity. (p. 64)

Reading is part of children's situated histories. Miller argues that readers and practices of reading are situated within histories of locality, gender, race, and class. Literacy learning is part of these histories, not something that children do as a cognitive task divorced from their lives. As she writes:

Children have never just learned how to read and write and then looked around for uses to which they might put these skills. As they learn to do these things they are also learning to engage with the culture and with specific and specialised practices in that culture. They are also learning about being children in this culture, and especially children who may be black, girls, working-class, poor. (Miller, 1990, p. 158)

When I think back to the richness and complexity of my own girlhood experiences, I am filled with words and images that do not readily fit within the discourses of cultural and critical literacy research. But of what value are the memories of that small history for those who study literacy? What is their value in shaping theory, research, and practice? These are questions that have guided me toward hybrid languages of inquiry that are as complicated as a young girl's struggles to make sense of some pretty powerful meanings and practices in her life. I have turned to the languages of literary memoirs to help shape a theory of reading reflective of the complexity of actual reading practices. Centering my analysis around these fictions, or literary shapings, of girlhood memories, I allow concrete experiences and attachments to surface in my text. Stories from my childhood and memoirs by literary writers become part of a textured analysis in which the details of the memoirs become the focal points of inquiry. As I write stories of growing up in a rural, blue-collar setting and engage with other memories of working-class girlhoods, I reflect on the meaning of such inquiries for understanding practices of reading. The details of the narratives are important to creating more complex understandings of how relations of gender and class play out in individuated histories of reading. Girlhood memories reveal very different relations of class, gender, and race, and their connections to reading. The narrated memories also emphasize response and imagination—girlhoods shaped within discourses but that also reshape those discourses.

I begin my analysis with two literary memoirs of girlhood experiences. Autobiographical texts by Janet Frame (a poet and novelist) and bell hooks (a literary theorist and feminist educator) were chosen in part because of their rich depictions of early reading practices. As I turn to my experiences growing up, shared themes of girlhood imagination and literary experience become apparent, as do the racial, material, and economic factors that created different histories of class and of reading. This more complicated view of gender and class relations is connected with Laurie's history of reading, as it is told in Chapter 4, and most importantly with the complexities of writing her history from a perspective informed by my life experiences. Throughout this chapter, I focus on how reading practices are lived by working-class girls.

MEMORIES OF GIRLHOOD

In her memoir, bell hooks (1996) uses literary form to convey her imaginings, resistances, dependencies, and longings as a girl growing up. *Bone Black* opens with prose that conveys a sense of the magic even in experiences situated in southern racism and painful family relationships. Using language rich in literary detail, hooks conveys the interplay of relations with caretakers; racial, economic, and material forces; and her imaginary life as a young girl:

> *Bone Black: memories of girlhood* is not an ordinary tale. It is the story of girlhood rebellion, of my struggle to create self and identity distinct from and yet inclusive of the world around me. Writing imagistically, I seek to conjure a rich magical world of southern black culture that was sometimes paradisical and at other times terrifying. While the narratives of family life

I share can be easily labeled dysfunctional, significantly that fact will never alter the magic and mystery that was present—all that was deeply life sustaining and life affirming. The beauty lies in the way it all comes together exposing and revealing the inner life of a girl inventing herself—creating the foundation of selfhood and identity that will ultimately lead to the fulfillment of her true destiny—becoming a writer. (p. xi)

hooks describes her girlhood struggles to invent herself in a rural Black community as connected with her relations with others. An important thread of identity and connection recounted in her memoir is her relationship with her mother. This was a complex relationship, not without its pain. hooks writes of the strong feelings between a headstrong little girl and a mother struggling to meet the economic and emotional needs of her family. The bonds of love between mother and daughter were complicated by hooks's reluctance to conform. Memories of girlhood are conveyed in language depicting strong attachments but sometimes disappointment and sadness for both mother and daughter. hooks writes of her special love for other women in her life—Big Mama, her great-great grandmother, and her grandmother, Saru. And yet her girlhood identities were also constructed in "manifestations of difference" (Miller, 1990) in relation to her brother. At first puzzled by those differences, hooks writes of her growing understanding that her worlds, and those of her older brother, were shaped within different value systems. She tells the story of fantasy play with a red wagon, in which she began to understand the gendered roles that had her ride in the wagon pulled by her brother. Her brother's life story was to shape him as a would-be prince, hooks narrates, whereas she would be the princess (p. 19).

Throughout her memoir, hooks recounts the ways that race and class intersected in her history. Her girlhood is set in the cultural and material context of southern racism, the divided society that shaped my own White working-class girlhood. Growing up as a working-class Black girl, hooks learns about race but struggles with its meanings for her. She is light-skinned, bone black as she later writes. Her understandings of race are intertwined with the complex meanings of Whiteness and Blackness in relationship with adults whose voices convey bitterness, fear, and perplexity. Those voices become aspects of her emerging identity, growing up in a world differentiated by race. Her memoir reflects an evolving understanding of that difference and her struggles to understand its complex meanings:

She has learned to fear white folks without understanding what it is she fears. There is always an edge of bitterness, sometimes hatred, in the grown-ups' voice when they speak of them but never any explanation. When she learns of slavery in school or hears the laughter in geography when they see the pictures of naked Africans—the word *savage* underneath the pictures—she does not connect it to herself, her family. She and the other children want to understand Race but no one explains it. They learn without understanding that the world is more a home for white folks than it is for anyone else, that black people who most resemble white folks will live better in the world. They have a grandmother who looks white who lives on a street where all the other people are white. She tells them things like a Black nigger is a no-good nigger, that her Papa looked like a white man but was a nigger. She never explains to them why she has married a man whose skin is the color of soot and other wonderful black things, things they love—shoe polish, coal, women in black slips. (pp. 31–32)

As her memoir continues, hooks writes of the sexual longings tied up with her developing identity as a young Black girl. She longs for a woman's sexuality, for black slips and dresses. "Black is a woman's color—that's what her mama tells her. You have to earn the right to wear the color black" (p. 32). Race, class, sexuality—all become connected threads of her history, her emerging identities in relation with others.

Fantasy is presented in hooks's memoir as part of a history set amid relations of femininity, racism, and poverty. She writes her history as one filled with imaginary thinking. The worlds around her, physical surroundings that resonate with the lush, mystical qualities of a southern locality, become part of her fantasy life. She befriends a green garden snake, turning the snake into a confidant. It is the snake who helps her sort through some of the difficult relationships she has with family members. The bright green creature is a benevolent other in the context of sometimes painful realities.

As hooks writes about becoming a reader, her memoir reveals the practices that shaped reading in a southern Black community. The caretakers and church elders in her community were central to that history, helping to form her young life as a reader within a specific place and time. For instance, hooks writes of an old man reading in church. His voice, his caring demeanor, his hand in hers as the two discussed her imaginary worlds—these were part of reading practices shared between little girl and older man:

One of those men walked with his body bent, crippled. The grown-ups frowned at her when she asked them why he didn't walk straight. Did he know how to walk straight? Had he ever learned? They never answered. Every Sunday he read the scripture for the main offering. His voice wrinkled like paper. Sometimes it sounded as if there were already tears in it waiting to spill over, waiting to wet the thirsty throats of parched souls. She could not understand the reading. Only one part was clear. It was as though his voice suddenly found a message that eased sorrow, a message brighter than any tear. It was the part that read, It is required and understood that a man be found faithful. He was one of the faithful.

She loved the sight of him. After church, she would go and stand near him, knowing that he would give her his hand, covered old bones in wrinkled brown skin that reminded her of a well-worn leather glove. She would hold that hand tight, never wanting to give it back. In a wee pretend voice full of tears and longing he would ask for his hand back saying all the while that he would love for her to keep it but could not build his house without it. She loved to hear him talk about the house that he had been building for years, a dream house, way out in the country, with trees, wildflowers, and animals. She wanted to know if there were snakes. He assured her that if she came to visit the snakes would come out of their hiding places just for her, singing and playing their enchanted flutes. (p. 65)

hooks writes that her history as a reader evolved partly in relation to her longing to escape a sometimes lonely, conflicted life in her family. Reading, fantasy, Blackness, femininity, sexuality, and a rebellious and isolated childhood were interconnected strands of her history. As she read, she searched for ways to connect her emerging life experiences with books. Like the benevolent green tree snake, books became her friends, her confidants, sources of pleasure and solace. She began to look for aspects of herself in literary texts and to shape her identities in engagements with books. As hooks's memoir goes on to tell us how she later began to experiment with writing, we see the uniqueness of this story of a developing young artist. And yet such engagements with literacies, involving concrete others who shape our earliest experiences, are aspects of how all children come to be readers—those who read and write as girls or boys, in class and racially specific locations, and with the caretakers who take their hands, sharing their fantasy worlds and creating shared histories in which reading is part of relations in an always-already social world.

Janet Frame's (1991) memoir of growing up in New Zealand offers, as does hooks's memoir, an unusually detailed account of becoming a young reader. This autobiographical account from a writer of fiction and poetry again shows the ways in which material relations and attachments with others shape early practices of reading. Volume I of Frame's autobiography, *To the Is-Land*, tells the story of a girlhood lived in near-poverty conditions in New Zealand at the time of the Depression. Frame's early home experiences were embedded in emotionally intense and sometimes painful family relationships. Her brother was ill with epilepsy. Her father was prone to angry outbursts, particularly when the stress of trying to provide for a family of six children became unbearable. However, like bell hooks, Janet Frame led an imaginative life that was later to become a valuable resource to her as a novelist and poet. Early on, she narrates, she created "adventures" connected to reading and writing. She discovered that she could reinvent everyday, mundane experiences and create new ones.

> That year [Standard One] I discovered the word *Island*, which in spite of all the teaching I insisted on calling Is-Land. In our silent reading class at school, when we chose one of the Whitcombes school readers, those thin, fawn-covered books with crude drawings on the cover and speckled pages, I found a story, *To the Island*, an adventure story that impressed me so much that I talked about it at home.
>
>   "I read a story, *To the Is-Land*, about some children going to an Is-Land."
>
>   "It's I-Land," Myrtle [her older sister] corrected.
>
>   "It's not," I said. "It's Is-Land. It says," I spelled the letters, "I-s-l-a-n-d. Is-land."
>
>   "It's a silent letter," Myrtle said. "Like knee."
>
>   In the end, reluctantly, I had to accept the ruling, although within myself I still thought of it as the Is-land.
>
>   I began reading more "adventure" books, realising that to have an adventure, I did not need to travel in the lost Lizzie Ford, getting sick on the way, to beaches and rivers—I could experience an adventure by reading a book. (p. 33)

As a young child, Frame's early reading experiences were ones that allowed her to connect personal adventures with the stories she encountered in New Zealand textbooks. Her literary worlds were also points of connection for her with friends and family. Still attending an infant school (roughly the equivalent of primary school), Frame borrowed a friend's copy of *Grimm's Fairy Tales*. This book was transformative for her as a young reader:

> That night I took *Grimm's Fairy Tales* to bed and began to read, and suddenly the world of living and the world of reading became linked in a way I had not noticed before. "Listen to this," I said to Myrtle and Dots and Chicks. They listened while I read "The Twelve Dancing Princesses", and as I read and they listened, I knew and they knew, gloriously, that *we* were the Dancing Princesses—not twelve but four; and as I read, I saw in my mind the place in the coat cupboard in the corner of the bedroom where we could vanish to the underground world and the orchard that was "our" orchard along the gully where the boughs of the trees honked and cried out when they were broken, silver and gold trees; and in the end it was Myrtle who married the old soldier who, in my mind, looked like Vincent, the man of twenty-

two, to us, shrivelled and old, who had fallen in love with Myrtle, who was barely twelve when she went for a holiday to the Wyndham Walkers. (p. 43)

Frame's emerging desire to be a reader and later on a writer is portrayed in her memoir not as an Is-land to itself, but connected to desires voiced by her mother. Though poor, her mother had a desire to be a writer, one that was never fully realized in the midst of meeting the needs of her large family. Writing about her preschool years, Frame describes her mother's efforts to publish her poetry: "It was then . . . that Mother began publishing her poems each week in the *Wyndham Farmer* and soon became known, with pride, as 'Lottie C. Frame, the local poet'" (p. 20).

Some of Frame's earliest memories include poems written and recited by her mother, often ones related to the New Zealand landscape in which they lived:

The lighthouse on the rocky shore
        the seagulls' lonely cry
and day departing leaves behind
        God's pictures in the sky. (p. 15)

Later on, when Frame began to write poetry in the railway book given to her by her father, and to contemplate becoming a poet herself, she saw her own desires and efforts as connected to a shared identity with her mother. She recalls keeping an index of her emerging poetry, reflecting on how her poetry was connected to the desires that her mother never saw fully realized:

My poems were a mixture of conventional ideas about "poetic" vocabulary and the cowboy and prison songs recorded in my other notebooks and the contents of the small popular song books brought home by Myrtle and the songs sung by my parents and grandparents. I continued writing my poems, sensing the approval of my parents—of Mother, who saw the birth of something she had mourned as lost from her life, whose overwhelming might-have-been was *publication* of a book. She once sent a collection of her poems to Stockwells, England, which advertised regularly in New Zealand newspapers and magazines, and her joy at having the poems accepted for publication was lessened only by the knowledge that she couldn't afford the sum of money they quoted for publication, and although she resigned herself to never having the money, she could say proudly now and again, "I've had a book of poems accepted for publication by Stockwells, Ilfracombe, England." (p. 76)

Emphasized in these autobiographical reflections are the ways in which one girl's identity as a reader and writer was shaped through relations with others. Moments of reading and writing and the desires that led to them are narrated as shared among family members and friends. Frame's relations with her mother are recounted as a key thread of her own history.

As I move now to reflect on my girlhood history of reading and writing, themes emerge that parallel these. Relations of class and gender played out in ways that I think are important to relate. The telling of a history I know so intimately is important for explaining the lens through which I came to understand Laurie's childhood. My girlhood experiences growing up in a specific class location became both a productive and a limiting vantage point for coming to know Laurie's experiences and problems in school. More similar in some ways to the early experiences of Janet Frame and bell hooks than to those of Laurie, my childhood engagements with literacy practices nonetheless became aspects of a teaching relationship. I allow those memories of girlhood to become part of a textured and critical analysis of gender, class, and literacy.

STORIES FROM A RURAL PAST

I grew up surrounded by stories. Sitting on the linoleum floor of the kitchen where my mother was often at work during my childhood, I listened to her stories of growing up in the Arkansas Delta. My childhood was partly shaped by these stories—her tales of growing up on a cotton plantation, living in a house on stilts, seeing her father go out on Saturday nights to help tenant families deal with a drunken man waving a gun, longing for the material goods and cultural richness she associated with a wealthy uncle. My summers growing up in a rural setting were spent listening to my mother's tales of past times, often ones expressing her desires to be classy, like those upper-class southerners she had once known. As a White woman growing up in a family with little money but high expectations for "manners" (social demeanor, dress codes), my mother longed for a classiness she associated with money. Her well-to-do uncle, who had made his money by purchasing cotton land and building ever-larger farms, had doted on her as a child. He brought her gifts, took her for rides in his car. He dressed in an elegant way. He was handsome, a real prince to her. As I grew up in a different southern kitchen, hearing my mother's memories of her childhood, I, too, began to long for the power that money can bring. I longed for the beautiful clothes, the handsome prince with a car. Fantasy was a means of creating alternative realities. My childhood history was shaped within stories that I now see as literary.

I spent much of my early childhood in a small town at the foot of the Blue Ridge Mountains. Though my family lived in town, the lives of town folks were informed by the surrounding rural landscape. Many townspeople had moved in from the hills descending in lush green folds from the mountain range that framed the region. We were cultural outsiders to this small town, having moved in for work connected to a satellite tracking station plopped on top of one of the higher hills. On work days (and sometimes nights for the graveyard shift), my father donned his brown technician's outfit and headed out to work. My mother stayed at home to cook and clean house. During the summers and after school, my brother and I were free to roam the roads (some paved and some dirt) leading from our street down to a small country store or up the hill to the laundromat owned by the family of a friend of mine. It was in this working-class town that I became a reader.

I have memories of working alongside my close friend who had to do her chores at the laundromat; of playing with Barbie dolls in the grassy area next to our house; of falling in love at age 6 with Paul McCartney; of getting lost in the woods with some friends who insisted that we could find some caves if we wandered far enough back into the hills. I remember the voices of locals talking about the hills and their mysteries—voices telling stories about ghosts and Big Foot and uttering warnings about snakes (*beat the bushes before walking into them*) mingled with the TV shows we watched and my mother's Delta version of southern ideology. These voices became part of a hybrid identity (as all identities are hybrid) formed in a unique time and regional location. I can remember the warmth of that time and place. The new preacher's house, brought to a state of dirty disarray by the former preacher's family, was cleaned and freshly painted by churchwomen. My mother wielded her paint brush as I played next to her and the other women, feeling the goodness emanating from these small-town practices of living. Other memories surface: memories of screams of terror as I realized I had planted my bare foot on top of a huge water moccasin (a snake feared by all in rural southeastern culture); memories of holding a jar of freshly captured fireflies that magically lit up a summer's night; memories of a lump in my heart as I listened to a story told by the Christian lady who lived down the street. The other day, she had told me, a Negro lady had said to her, sobbing, that she wished she had never been born because she was Black. Memories of the dark mysticism of the Blue Ridge Mountains and the rhythms of a country song—these, too, were part of a history as rich and complex as those recounted by hooks and Frame.

I didn't grow up in a home with a lot of books. My family subscribed to a service that mailed us some children's Golden Books once in a while. My mother used these and a few other anthologies she had purchased to read to my brother and me each night. These bedtime readings became for me aspects of an imaginary universe that seemed as ordinary as everyday life. Stories about Pegasus the flying horse, showing pictures of the beautiful winged creature flying into the clouds and guided by the handsome Bellerophon, mingled with a childhood imagination fed by the mystical landscape around me and my mother's gift for storytelling. I freely invented stories as I played with Barbie dolls and small plastic animals, and wandered down the streets that connected our wood frame house to the store where local men sat out front, or to the laundromat where I sometimes played. These roads led to other spaces, too. My mother had once lived in the *city* as a young working woman. She told stories of the excitement of her city life, stories filled with longing for those past times. On big shopping trips, we took a winding highway leading out of town to the nearby city, Asheville. The magic of those shopping trips was part of the pleasure that fantasy, and city life, provided.

Unlike Janet Frame's memories of her earliest reading experiences, I do not have vivid memories of learning to read. I know that reading in general was something people did in school, or maybe in certain workplaces. Adults didn't typically sit around the house reading, except for a magazine or two. Reading was also something that was expected to be *taught* in school—few children read before going to first grade. As a young girl, I read and did spelling and other writing tasks in order to please my teachers—to be a "good girl" in school. As things turned out, I was quite successful in that role. I quickly became known as a smart girl who didn't cause the teachers any trouble. This is a dual identity that Walkerdine (1990) describes as one of the ways girls can be successful in school. Smart girls who are also "nice and helpful" can attain high classroom status. This was a costly identity for me, though, growing up as I did in a rural setting. In such working-class localities, being smart and female can carry its share of pain, as well as classroom success. I found myself turning to literary stories in ways that mirrored my mother's recalled past and imagined future: as a means of escape from realities that were not always embracing of my differences.

A memory comes to mind of reading a social studies textbook, perhaps in third or fourth grade. This textbook had a story in it, a narrative that I would now view as a kind of fictional anthropology with some geography thrown in. This selection in our textbook described the life of a little boy living on a faraway tropical island. I remember sitting at my desk, becoming immersed in this imagined tropical place. I pictured myself there, living in this exotic land, like the child in the story. For those magical moments of reading, I was living beyond the limits of a fairly old school building and its daily monotony.

As for Janet Frame, the worlds of living and the worlds of reading came together easily for me. Thinking back on those early years of reading, I can see these two worlds coming together around a love of imaginary places, a longing for something that would transport me from the sometimes mundane quality of everyday life. For all its romance to outsiders, life in a country town can be pretty boring. As outsiders who had moved into this physically beautiful setting, my family and I were also an isolated nuclear unit of social and cultural life. The kinship networks that sustained local life—the cousins, aunts, uncles, and grandparents who were always nearby—were missing from our lives in town. I figured out how to entertain myself in a setting where I was often playing alone, or in the house near my mother as she worked on getting dinner ready or on house chores. I don't believe that I saw the worlds of reading and the worlds of imaginative play as separate. I could live stories in my imagination as I played in the field next to our house and as I read selections from the Golden Books displayed in our living room. These were parallel forms of imaginative practice, and I made no special effort to read as opposed to doing something equally interesting. In school, though, these worlds could easily merge as I experienced moments of pleasure within a story.

Such moments of pleasure in school were limited. Like the working-class schooling practices that Patrick Finn (1999) critiques in *Literacy with an Attitude*, I experienced school as a set of routine tasks. A memory surfaces: It is the first day of school in second grade. I have been assigned to a veteran second-grade teacher whom everyone raves about. She instructs our class, seated in individual desks lined up in rows, to copy a paragraph off the blackboard, in *pen*. So anxious to please my new teacher, to show her what a good student I am, I copy the paragraph as neatly as I can, in my best handwriting.

These traditional practices of literacy, not all that different from ones that shape the learning experiences of working-class children today, did a lot to teach me the values associated with being a successful schoolgirl: obedience, accuracy, conformity, work. I worked hard at school, as school was seen as work. Few of the metaphors of play associated with progressive education, and with middle-class practices of child rearing (see Walkerdine, 1984), touched my experiences with reading and writing in school. Children went to school to work and to do what the teachers told them to do, just as adults accepted that everyday work was often routine, boring, and controlled by others. What did happen for me, though, were transgressive moments, perhaps unknown to others, where the pleasures of imaginary thinking and of reading came together. This happened with writing, too, but only rarely. I recall a time much later (probably in fourth or fifth grade) when a teacher allowed my class to make up a story—to compose our own written narrative. I remember the feeling of giddy anticipation and freedom this evoked for me as I set off to write a fictional story.

Femininity was for me connected to a classiness that exceeded the material realities of our lives. With the proliferation of fashion magazines and TV shows, media images of femininity were readily available even to those living in small towns. My mother appropriated these images of middle-class femininity even as she engaged in others that reflected the values of small-town life. She would easily go to the local A&P grocery store in curlers but insist on dressing up to go to a school function. I have a memory of a Christmas play in which I was performing the part of an angel. My mother came to the classroom wearing an attractive black wool dress and a string of imitation pearls. I felt a sense of pride and belonging—here was my mother, looking so classy as she came to watch me perform. Feminine classiness was one of the strongest values impressed upon me. This was a value that allowed my mother and her mother to transgress the material limits of their lives. My mother had grown up poor in the Arkansas Delta. However, her family had *class*. Her mother, a southern beauty, had married a man of good moral standing, a man who was later to oversee farms worked by Black men living with their families as tenant farmers. This position of farm manager, along with his moral character in general, enabled my mother's father to provide well for his family. Partly with the help of her well-off uncle, my mother dressed well. Her mother bought nice clothes, too, and she had decent furniture. They lived *between* classes—with limited economic means but desires to live in fashionable ways even in the context of a southern Delta town.

I was raised within similar values. However, the dynamics of material goods, classiness, and femininity played out differently in my childhood. Economically, we were better off than my mother had been in her childhood. Though we started off in very meager circumstances, living at first with my maternal grandmother, my father's steady work enabled us to move gradually toward getting some of the things my mother, in particular, wanted for her family. We went to the small city nearby to buy clothes for school, putting coats and more expensive items on layaway. As she herself had experienced as a girl, we lived in ways that sometimes exceeded the material conditions of our lives. Scrupulously saving for shopping trips, putting away something each month in a Christmas fund, we lived the classiness my mother associated with a good life. On Easter, my brother and I were dressed to the hilt. On Christmas, I awoke to a room full of new Barbie dolls and their many accoutrements. Difficult to assign to a single class label, this was a girlhood lived between values and economic practices. I think I would have been lost in a setting in which there was real money. Still, elegance was sometimes part of small-town life—even if for the brief moment of a Christmas play or an Easter Sunday church service.

These family values were complicated by the fact that my mother had married a man with different values. So divergent from the southern emphasis on manners and classiness my mother had known as a girl, my father's family was problematic for her. His family was, within those Delta practices of living, not a "good family" with strong values and good manners. In some ways, at least for my mother's family, she had married beneath the expectations for a marriage that solidifies, even increases, one's social standing. My mother had married for love, but love spread out over years of material struggle and family conflict can carry its emotional costs as well as its joys. Increasingly, as my two young parents struggled to make ends meet and raise a family, their differences overtook the romance that had fueled my mother's willingness to leave the safety and warmth of her own family and the vibrancy of living in a big southern city. Pregnant with her first child, my mother followed her new husband out to a navy base in California. What ensued were years of struggle and often pain, as two very different people attempted to raise their children within ideologies that never quite came together. My mother saw her identity as connected to what might have been as well as what was.

A memory from my childhood: My mother tells me stories of her romantic escapades in high school. She was, according to her telling of things, greatly desired by young men. She was, during the latter days of high school, dating one of the more attractive boys in her small town, a football player with thick dark hair, a handsome Italian-looking face, and a muscular body. She shows me an old picture depicting him in a football pose. She tells the story of a night out on the town. She was hanging out with her girlfriends, smoking in a small-town diner. Her handsome boyfriend came along and begged her to go out with him, to date him exclusively and seriously. She drew long and hard on her cigarette and slowly blew the smoke into the room. "I'll think about it," she told him, within hearing range of all present. She tells me this story in the context of pointing out the romantic opportunities she had as a girl growing up. A lesson often attached to such stories of romance and seduction was the importance of getting the right man. My mother often talked about her youthful romances as a means of warning me about mistakes, of pointing out what could have been. Many men were pursuing her when, as a young woman, she later lived and worked in a large southern city. She had men begging her to date and even marry. Her own mother had urged her to consider one of them, whom she ultimately turned down. She did not have to marry the man she did, my mother often told me. Romantic princes had courted her. Stories of romantic princes and smoky seductions were fictions my mother shared with me, stories that shaped my childhood.

In some respects, my father's values reflected traditional male practices. On Sundays, he would stay at home and watch football as my mother got the kids ready and went off to church. He worked around the house on weekends and kept things running, while my mother did all the cooking, housecleaning, and child care. He was an intellectually curious man for someone who had himself grown up in poverty. He enjoyed history and informative TV shows. When push came to shove, however, he was the one who held onto certain values my mother rejected. He thought the purchase of nice clothes extravagant and unnecessary. His angry tone of voice toward children reflected a style of child rearing my mother found offensive. He could be abrasive and even brutal, holding nothing back, as would the southern men who had shaped my mother's girlhood history.

In this family and small-town setting, I embraced the class identity my mother desired, and I longed for a kind of middle-class femininity my father in some ways rejected. Though I loved both parents as a child, my education was shaped more within a value context connected with my mother. This is not an uncommon set of relations between gender and class identities. Even in working-class and poor families, women often aspire to the images of femininity projected in the media. Girls' identities are shaped within these multiple relations—their love for their mothers, their mothers' desires to live beyond their material limits and social-class standing. Strings of fake pearls get mixed up with educational aspirations as young girls aim to be something more than money can immediately provide. Relations with fathers can get caught up in this desire for classiness connected with money, femininity, and education.

Annie Ernaux writes about such dynamics in her memoirs about her father (1992) and her mother (1991)—working-class parents living in Normandy. She describes the "fractured love" (1992, p. 13) that emerged as part of a web of relations involving social class, gender, language, and education. As she began to define herself as a girl who was successful with middle-class schooling, she became aware of differences in the discourses and identities of home and school. Her relations with her father became more strained with the realization of the "broadness" of his language, even though he took pains to speak proper French. Tones of voice and forms of language evoking certain values became for her associated with a growing separation from the ways of life practiced by her father. Growing up with him, Ernaux found Norman French to be part of an intimacy made more complex by gendered differences that were refracted through language practices:

> At home, when we spoke to one another, it was always in a querulous tone of voice. Only strangers were entitled to polite behavior. The habit was so deep-rooted that my father—who applied himself to speaking properly in front of other people—would automatically revert to Norman French and to his broad accent and aggressive tone whenever he told me not to climb on the heap of rubble in the yard. This ruined his efforts to create a good impression. He always used popular speech when he scolded me. Besides, if he had spoken properly, I would never have taken seriously his threats about slapping me. (1992, p. 60)

Ernaux writes of her relations with her mother somewhat differently. Though working-class and rural Norman traditions were no less an influence in her mother's life, Ernaux writes of her mother's aspirations toward middle-class social conventions, especially education. She forged a close relationship with her mother around learning and her mother's quest for bettering one's existence, for becoming a cultivated member of society:

> She longed to learn the rules of good behavior and was always worrying about social conventions, fearful of doing the wrong thing. She longed to know what was in fashion, what was new, the names of famous writers, the recent films on release—although she didn't go to the cinema, she hadn't time—and the names of flowers in the gardens. She listened attentively when people spoke of something she didn't know, out of curiosity, and also because she wanted to show that she was eager to learn. In her opinion, self-improvement was first and foremost a question of learning, and nothing was more precious than knowledge. . . . I thought her a cut above my father because she seemed closer to the schoolmistresses and teachers than he did. Everything about my mother—her authority, her hopes, and her ambitions—was geared to the very concept of education. We shared an intimacy centered on books, the poetry I read to her and the pastries in the teashop at Rouen, from which he was excluded. (1991, pp. 45–46)

In my girlhood history, desires for classiness were also connected with school and learning. Aiming to please my father as well, someone who had always wanted to study history and other subjects, I increasingly became a model student. My goodness was lived through my schoolwork, which my parents viewed with a pride they shared. The love that did bind us in these early years of school, however, became, as Ernaux would describe things, fractured. Often concerned with my older brother, who was a problematic child, my parents struggled to keep intact a family that was hanging together by increasingly fragile threads. Perhaps intent on creating my own Is-Land of pleasure and acceptance, I turned to school as a way out of a painful family life and a rural-town existence I often found boring. I grew to hate the Sunday afternoons that stretch on and on in small-town life. As a girl growing up, I found the details of life told in fictional stories increasingly interesting. I longed to live those fictions, even to write them. By the time I reached high school, I was writing poetry in addition to getting As on my assigned schoolwork. Though my history as a reader and writer was to take a different course from my mother's history, I drew on her imagined worlds. My worlds of little girlhood and young adolescence were shaped within stories she taught me to value. I reworked these into a narrative of departure as I separated myself more and more from small-town life.

Class relations, gender, and school practices are lived in ways that are fluid, not easily confined to more reductive categories of analysis. Narratives are suited to elaborating the web of relations that make up individuated histories of reading and writing. Gender and class can be viewed through the nuance of practices that are felt as well as cognitively known. Girls can be portrayed as complex subjects who assert their agencies, even as their lives are shaped within relations of material goods, affective ties with others, and practices of schooling. My life as a young reader was perhaps unique in ways that resemble the experiences of bell hooks and Janet Frame. Memories of girlhood are for me connected to an unusual configuration of forces that led toward reading and writing as forms of imaginative activity. Still, all childhood histories are as complex as those recounted in these memoirs of girlhood, social class, and reading—situated within hybrid identities and sometimes conflicted relations with others. I have aimed toward a style of writing that illuminates those details, highlighting the way literacy practices are lived by subjects. As I turn to a reading of another working-class girlhood, I demonstrate how these remembered images, feelings, and literacies are connected with an analysis that is, after all, a situated one.

READINGS OF A WORKING-CLASS GIRLHOOD

Laurie was adamant during the time that I knew her that she wanted to be a writer and an artist. My earliest memories of Laurie in kindergarten are of her at work at the Writing Center. Children were free to choose Centers in kindergarten, and Laurie often chose the Writing Center. She made card lists of friends and drawings. In May of her kindergarten year Laurie commented, while at work on a self-portrait at the Art Center, that she wanted to be an artist when she grew up. On two later occasions, she took a moment to remind me of her love of writing and drawing. "You know, I like to draw and write. Remember?" she commented while writing a story in the spring of first grade. These comments seemed to reflect back on an earlier time, perhaps to kindergarten. "You remember how I used to write a lot?" she noted on another occasion. However, her reflections also projected a fantasy about the adult woman she would become. In second grade, in response to a journal-writing activity, Laurie wrote, "When I grow up I want to be a rtr and artest."

Laurie also connected easily with literature, and she had a strong understanding of story genres and forms. On one of my regular home visits in second grade, I brought along a copy of a picture storybook I thought she might enjoy. *Where's Our Mama* is a children's storybook with repetitive text and an engaging story about two young girls who are lost in turn-of-the-century Paris. With the help of a police officer, the two girls search for their mama among the different women they encounter on Parisian streets and in shops and businesses:

> "Is this your mama?"
>
> "Oh, no, sir. Our mama doesn't read the newspaper. Mama reads books—millions of books."
>
> "Is this your mama?"
>
> "Oh, no, sir. Our mama never whispers. Everyone loves mama's voice—she is famous for it."

I first read this book aloud to Laurie, since she had missed a whole-class reading because she was attending her Chapter One reading program. I suggested to Laurie that we read the book together the second time around; she seemed hesitant to try the book on her own. She latched on to a phrase from the book, "Ooh la la!" Laurie and I were reading outside, since it was a warm fall afternoon. Shortly after our joint reading, she took a colorful umbrella lying near her lawn chair and held it over her head, seemingly in a nod to the turn-of-the-century elegance of ladies depicted in the book's illustrations. She began dancing on the front lawn, turning in circles with her umbrella extended and chanting gleefully, "Ooh la la! Ooh la la!" At moments like these, the worlds of living and the worlds of reading came together for Laurie.

Literacy, however, was the academic area in which Laurie was to become most vulnerable in school. Although teacher and researcher observations of Laurie in kindergarten indicated solid strengths in literacy, by the middle of first grade it was apparent that she was falling seriously behind. When in the middle of first grade her difficulties began to be painfully obvious, I began working with her after school and, later on, in the summer. During my visits, we read children's books together, and she drew and wrote stories. She often drew on themes from the books we read as she composed her own stories. She was, at least in the early years of school, a stronger and more confident writer than reader. I hoped that a combination of writing, drawing, and reading during my one-on-one work with Laurie would empower her, giving her greater confidence as a struggling reader and writer. She and I formed a relationship around practices of reading and writing.

As my work with Laurie progressed across her first- and second-grade years in school, shared strands of imaginative thinking, family relations, and feminine identities emerged as part of our relationship. Laurie was growing up amid sometimes painful family dynamics. These became points of identification for me, as did her ways of weaving imaginary fictions into everyday life. Laurie seemed, as I had been as a young girl, enchanted with exotic, otherworldly images of tropical worlds and magic gardens with mythical creatures. On a muggy afternoon in the summer following first grade, we made our way into a grassy park near the laundromat where she spent summer days. Laurie imagined trees in an adjacent wooded area to be a tropical rain forest. She noted that some of these "tropical" trees could be banana trees. At other times, Laurie wrote and drew fictional stories involving magic gardens inhabited by flowers, fairies, unicorns, and devilish creatures. I searched for books connected to her interests as we created a shared interest in gardens and mythical creatures in them. In late summer following first grade, we took a trip to a formal garden where for a day we walked amid fountains, ponds, tropical trees, flowers, and outdoor cafes. Working in a grassy playground near the Laundromat where Laurie spent summer days with her grandmother, we made thistle-flower necklaces and bracelets when taking a break from the more strenuous demands of reading and writing. Images of girlhood, reading and writing, and fantasy intersect with images of a Laundromat set in a working-class neighborhood. I thought I understood some of the difficulties that Laurie faced, and I reached out to help her change an emerging course of school failure.

In January of Laurie's second-grade year, we made a trip together to Borders Bookstore. We had at that point done some hard work over the summer and into second grade. I had been trying to help Laurie build up a repertoire of books she could call her own. She had read on her own the books I selected for each home visit. As an incentive for her hard work, she had been filling up a Borders "Young Readers Club" book purchase card. She got a sticker for each book she read independently. On a chilly winter afternoon after school, we headed off to Borders to reap the rewards of her efforts.

As we made our way to Borders, I was struck by the ways in which our two histories intersected around certain themes. My readings of Laurie's experiences were refracted through the lens of my girlhood history, as I was coming to realize. My reflective journal writing addressed the teaching relations that connected two childhood histories.

> On the way to Borders, we drove into a lovely evening winter scene, with the sun setting amid wispy clouds and the icy waters covered with feeding seagulls. Laurie began to talk about the clouds as if they were different mythical creatures, like unicorns and Pegasus the flying horse. I shared with her that the story of Pegasus was my favorite story when I was growing up as a little girl. I felt so connected to Laurie at this moment. Her imagination was working in much the same way as mine had worked to weave fantasies out of a sometimes bland, if not harsh, reality. Money was in short supply at home, but the clouds could still turn into mythical flying creatures. There was the possibility of escape. I wanted so desperately to make this trip one of escape, no doubt because of my connection with Laurie, my feelings about her. I remembered the times that I would go with my mother to the larger city near where I had grown up in a small southern town. On these shopping trips, centered on material things—the objects of my mother's desires and mine—my worlds that often felt so closed and bland would explode with possibilities. The buildings around us were bigger and more elegant. They offered the promise of something larger, nicer than the everyday world. I think in some inarticulate way I wanted Laurie to have this same kind of experience—the experience of leaving the sometimes difficult realities of her everyday worlds and living, even if momentarily, in something that evoked fantasy—but was also real, tangible. We found Borders Bookstore, and I immediately suggested that we head to the cafe. (Fieldnotes)

Common themes did shape our two histories of girlhood—themes of femininity in a class context, mother–daughter attachments, and fantasy. However, the ways these themes intersected with school literacy practices differed to a degree that I can only now, with the distance that time provides, fully appreciate. Though Laurie clearly wanted to be a reader and a writer, the subject positions these new practices entailed were more difficult for her. She resisted those practices as strongly as she embraced our work together, and as desperately as she wanted to be a "good girl" in school. Other kinds of desire shaped her schoolgirl history in relation to those she loved more than me, and more than her teachers. Laurie identified strongly with her mother, even though relations with her mother were at times difficult. Though she seemed to know how to push the buttons of an often tired, stressed-out young mother, her identifications with her mother were as important as those that shaped my girlhood and those of Janet Frame and bell hooks. Mother–daughter relations were formed around histories of academic struggle in school, and longings for a prince who would bring love, happiness, and material comforts. Stories of romance shaped Laurie's girlhood, but in different ways than were true of my childhood. She embraced the seductions of romance and domesticity, turning to these as more vibrant possibilities than academic success. Resistance to adults, flirtation with boys, academic struggles, and being a "good girl" in the classroom—these became strands of a young reader's history as I came to know it.

Michel de Certeau (1984) argues that narrated histories create fictional spaces. They are, as he suggests, *narrations*, not descriptions (p. 79). Choices of style and form create different literary experiences. They evoke different feelings and different relations between writer and reader, author and subject. Laurie's story of becoming a reader and writer in grades K–2 is a complicated one for me to write because I was at times a part of that story. Not to allow those points of connection to be visible would create a more dishonest text. The fact was that I tried to do everything I could to change Laurie's chances for becoming a strong reader and writer. I also identified with her and used experiences from my girlhood as points from which to construct a teaching relationship with her. This unique set of conditions became a small part of her history as a reader and writer in school, and it is part of my telling of that history. I occasionally allow a more intimate voice—expressing frustration, bewilderment, caring—to surface in the stories I tell. Typically concealed in the arts of writing literacy research, attachments and identifications are part of teaching relations. Teaching, like research, involves situated readings of students. We read students' lives in ways that draw on our own histories as learners. The fictional spaces that I create in Chapter 4 are reflective of these truths of everyday practice.

❧ 4 ❧

Fictions of Girlhood

I begin to want things I've never wanted before: braids, a dressing gown, a purse of my own. Something is unfolding, being revealed to me. I see that there's a whole world of girls and their doings that has been unknown to me, and that I can be part of it without making effort at all. I don't have to keep up with anyone, run as fast, aim as well, make explosive noises, decode messages on cue. I don't have to think about whether I've done these things well, as well as a boy. All I have to do is sit on the floor and cut frying pans out of the Eaton's Catalogue with embroidery scissors, and say I've done it badly. Partly this is a relief.

—Margaret Atwood, *Cat's Eye*

AS A YOUNG GIRL, Laurie faced a real juggling act in school. Growing up in a household with strong, hardworking women, she identified with the values she was learning from them. Laurie embraced the emotional and physical vibrancy of her young mother as her maternal grandmother provided warmth and sometimes set limits for Laurie's behavior. Her early years in school were intertwined with these primary identifications and their connections to the new academic practices Laurie would encounter. Influencing both home and school practices of living and learning were the economic hardships that she and her family lived from day to day. The stress of making ends meet while caring for three young children took its toll on the women who were Laurie's caretakers—and ultimately on Laurie's history in school. Laurie's mother and grandmother shared

---

The title of this chapter alludes to Valerie Walkerdine's book, *Schoolgirl Fictions*. This intertextual connection is appropriate, since in this chapter I am especially indebted to Walkerdine's important contributions to education, feminist theory, and critical psychology.

financial and child-care responsibilities, so that her mother could work and pursue college studies. Still, things were tough financially. Laurie's grandmother managed a laundromat during the day and worked a second job as well. Her mother worked nearly full time and went to school in the evenings while also caring for Laurie and her younger sister and brother.

Laurie was deeply loved by the two women who made great personal sacrifices to care for her. Still, within the bustle of activity taking place in her small, one-story home, Laurie struggled to get the emotional attention she wanted and needed. When things didn't work out for her at home, she acted out in enraged, even violent, ways. Her behavior at home was to lead ultimately to a medical diagnosis that was becoming widespread at the time of this research study: attention deficit disorder (ADD). The diagnosis was entangled in a history lived within material stresses and the emotional strain that went with them. Economic hardship, anger, and later struggles with academic practices were strands of the realities that Laurie lived and the important attachments she formed with her mother. How those threads of identity and action were interpreted and sometimes reinvented by Laurie is part of my telling of her history in primary school.

Laurie's history includes a prominent fiction that helped to shape her emerging schoolgirl identities. In the midst of tensions at home and, beyond kindergarten, at school, Laurie dreamed of a prince—a daddy who would bring love and material support, and boys who would be her special classroom friends. Her history as a reader and writer unfolds in relation to fictions such as these—ones shared with her mother, a woman in her 20s who was involved in a long-term romantic relationship when Laurie was in primary school. As early as kindergarten, Laurie formed coupled partnerships in which she could participate in a young girl's version of discourses of feminine attraction. A young boy became her special friend in kindergarten, and she appeared bolstered by the relationship she formed with him. This story of kindergarten friendship did not, however, forecast academic empowerment. Though Laurie appeared confident and even at times brazen in kindergarten, by first grade a different history was to emerge. Something Laurie also shared with her mother—difficulty with reading practices in school—increasingly impacted her classroom life as academic demands intensified in first and second grade. Sulky resistances in kindergarten that seemed minor at the time became more frequent, and yet also more subtle and concealed from others as Laurie matured socially.

Laurie's schoolgirl history is full of seeming contradictions as she learned to negotiate what Walkerdine (1990) describes as the splitting associated with being a feminine subject. As a young working-class girl, Laurie juggled her desires for love and social acceptance as she tried to figure out her place within tensions—being a good girl and acting out violently, becoming a model student and yet struggling with reading, being liked by boys and girls while dealing with her increasing vulnerabilities as a student. I embed her history as a reader in these multilayered and sometimes conflicting relations, attempting to understand *reading* as practices within them.

KINDERGARTEN ROMANCE AND RESISTANCE

It is hard to envision Laurie in kindergarten without thinking of Nicholas. During a child review (see Carini, 1982) constructed at the end of Laurie's kindergarten year with her teacher, Mrs. Thompson, and a research assistant, Hope Longwell-Grice, the word *symbiotic* came out as descriptive of their relationship. Laurie's teacher shared that she could not remember a time when they were not together as a couple. Laurie's relationship with Nicholas was both visible and public, and private. Everyone in the classroom knew about their closeness. Other children made comments like "Nicholas loves Laurie." If another child tried to sit next to Laurie when Nicholas had claimed the spot, he was quick to reclaim his position next to her. They worked and played together regularly during Centers time. However, when asked about Nicholas, an aura of secrecy emerged as part of how Laurie constructed herself within this relationship. In January, I was sitting next to Laurie at the Writing Center. Since I had my tape recorder close at hand, I asked her to narrate her story and I offered to take dictation. She narrated a story in which Nicholas was a fictional character:

> My baby sister is inside the house, and my pet dog is being shot. Nicholas is trying to build a house. I'm cutting grass. By the house lived an evil witch. She took people and cooked 'em and turned 'em into bread cookies.

Her drawing also depicted a small figure (representing Nicholas) next to the house and a baby inside. When I began to write this story onto her paper, however, she staunchly refused to have Nicholas's name mentioned. Later that year, I asked Laurie who her special friends in the classroom were. She looked at me with a shy smile and said, "You know who."

In the year's end review of Laurie's kindergarten progress, Mrs. Thompson, Hope Longwell-Grice, and I tried to make sense of this important relationship. What did it mean for the two children involved? How did it speak to Laurie's strengths as well as vulnerabilities in school? Initially, what emerged from our teacher–researcher dialogue was an emphasis on how Laurie assumed a domestic role in relation to Nicholas. Earlier in the year, Laurie had sometimes voiced a type of bossy presence in the classroom. In the case of Nicholas, this spilled over into an ethic of caretaking. Nicholas was a needy student; he struggled academically and had a social position that was weaker in relation to some of the more dominant children. Laurie, on the other hand, brought to her kindergarten classroom a history of assuming a motherly role at home. In my earliest visits to her home, during which time her youngest sibling was only a toddler and her sister 3 years old, she attended to her siblings as a caretaker. Several times during one visit, she made reference to how she was "the mom around here." In her interactions with Nicholas, she alternated between an adolescent-like identity and a motherly or domestic one.

For instance, in one videotaped episode, Laurie and Nicholas were working at a Center devoted to goop: a homemade cornstarch-and-water substance similar to Play-Doh. Different objects had been placed on the goop table, including some cups and spoons. A little girl sitting at the table with Laurie and Nicholas rolled out some goop patties and placed them against her face, feeling their composition and coolness. Laurie attended to Nicholas and to what he was doing with the goop. The two of them entered into a social interaction that resembled a domestic scene. Laurie spooned goop into cups as though cooking. She made some things herself and helped Nicholas sort through how to make things with his goop. She helped him when his goop stuck to the bottom of the cups he was using.

Though Laurie often assumed a caretaking stance toward Nicholas, she also engaged in flirtations with him, sometimes following *his* lead. In December of her kindergarten year, Laurie made a comical fuss about children dipping their cookies into their juice in the midst of snacktime. Nicholas was among the children dipping his cookies, and Laurie said teasingly, "I'll never sit by Nicholas again." Much later in the year another boy in the room commented that he had once seen Nicholas eat a worm. Laurie responded, "Yes, he's disgusting isn't he?" Though feigning disgust at some of Nicholas's behaviors and representing them as vulgar or repulsive, she hung close to him. During a symbolic play episode videotaped in the spring, Laurie and Nicholas were playing with some wooden vehicles in the blocks area. Laurie followed closely as Nicholas took the lead in negotiating the symbolic play. When another child tried to enter into the play space, Nicholas and Laurie resolutely shut him out by ignoring him. Nicholas and Laurie played for some time with the wooden vehicles, and then Nicholas moved on to build something with blocks. Laurie stood nearby, playing with Nicholas's hair, remaining at his side rather than engaging with the blocks herself. At our year-end analytical review of Laurie's kindergarten progress, Hope Longwell-Grice captured our collective reading of this episode: Stand by your man.

When the research study resumed in first grade, I was surprised to learn that Nicholas had changed schools. I was curious about how Laurie would respond to this change, since in kindergarten her social worlds had been so tightly constructed around Nicholas. In first grade, her social relations with peers did appear more dispersed. However, she also fancied herself in a relationship with a second boy, Steven. I first learned about Laurie's feelings for Steven during the spring months of first grade. During a regular home visit in April, Laurie and I were sitting at the kitchen table in her home, doing some reading and writing. There was a small vase of roses, mixed in with some baby's breath, on the table. Laurie commented that Steven had given her the small white flowers. She added that another girl in her classroom liked Steven, but that he liked only Laurie. I assumed that at least some of these narrated events were imaginary. More important to me than being truth or fantasy were the ways in which Laurie appropriated feminine discourses, casting herself in a gendered role in which she was the recipient of boys' romantic interest.

Academically, this girlhood identity was both productive and limiting for Laurie. She had seemed stronger and more confident in kindergarten than at any other time in her school history. At times, she became downright brassy, barking orders to Nicholas (who could be relatively naive, in her view) and letting other children know exactly how she felt about choices presented by her teacher. This social confidence easily spilled over into her academic work at Centers and other instructional areas. Part of the relationship she constructed with Nicholas focused on her stronger academic skills. She was academically and socially more mature than he was, and this gave her an edge of authority. However, the feminine identity that Laurie readily appropriated also sometimes limited her engagements in academic activities. The goop episode is illustrative. While the role of domestic partner gave Laurie power, it also limited her involvement in what was supposed to be an academic practice. Laurie's teacher wanted children to explore the physical properties of goop—as one girl demonstrated, to feel its properties of wetness and stickiness and even wonder about its composition. The academic practices that were intended to occur in the Centers were on many occasions appropriated within a domestic agenda.

Emergent Literacies

Laurie's embracing of traditional feminine roles during Centers activities
didn't impede her engagement in literacy practices. Literacy stood out as
an area of academic strength for Laurie in kindergarten. As noted earlier,
the Writing Center, a round table with writing tools and paper of assorted
sizes, colors, and shapes, was a favorite choice of hers. Images from
December of her kindergarten year evoke her frequent work at the Writing
Center during Centers time: Laurie is drawing a picture of her house.
She points out to me (observing and writing fieldnotes near her) that the
picture depicts her with her mom, having a barbecue. She turns to the
second page of her "book" (two pages stapled together) and begins writing. I ask her what she is writing, and if she would like for me to write
down the story she is telling with her picture. She responds that she is
going to be a writer. She begins writing strings of words and letters,
including the ABCs, words from books (there are some children's books
in a bookcase behind her), *I L U* (I love you), and the words from a book
that a classmate has begun to scan (*Chicka Chicka Boom Boom*).

Laurie seemed similarly confident with reading practices. According
to the assessments performed by her teacher at the beginning of the year,
Laurie did not enter kindergarten with strong alphabetic or numerical
understandings. In September she was only able to read accurately ap-
proximately half of the printed alphabet. However, she made rapid progress during the year. By January, she was able to read printed alphabet
letters (upper- and lower-case) with nearly 100% accuracy. Moreover,
Laurie seemed solidly familiar with literary discourses—the textual
shapes and structures of essayist discourse (see Scollon & Scollon, 1981)
that are crucial to reading and writing school-like texts. Her pretend-
reading of *The Valentine Bears*, audiotaped in February, suggests her relative ease with such discourses in kindergarten.

> LAURIE: there was a, the three little bears
> CHILD SEATED NEXT TO HER ON RUG: the three *big* bears
> LAURIE: three, one, two big bears
>> And Mrs. Bear woke up
>> And she uhm, and she set the clock on two
>> And she went outside in the deep (unclear word)
>> And she said, "brrrrr, it's cold"
>> Then, then she, and then she tried to wake Mr. Bear
>> She took a *cup* and filled it with water
>> Then she brung it inside

CHILD ON RUG: and then the bear reprised [sic] her
LAURIE: and the bear reprised her
    And the water splashed on *her*

In her pretend-bookreading, Laurie represents some textual relationships using intonation, a discourse strategy more typical of oral language than literary prose. Nonetheless, she makes use of what Scollon and Scollon (1981) refer to as *essayist* discourse in her representations of third-person characters ("Mrs. Bear woke up"), her use of literary phrasing ("there was three little bears"), and her representation of character speech ("and she said, 'brrrrr, it's cold'"). Laurie's pretend-reading draws formally and stylistically from literary texts, suggesting an incipient form of what Gordon Wells (1986) describes as a sense of story.

These engagements in literacy practices seemed to forecast a smooth transition into first-grade activities. Laurie seemed ready at that time to move into more textually focused activities such as writing and emergent reading. She was drawn to the Writing Center and expressed a desire to be a writer. She was confident about creating a verbal narrative when pretend-reading, and she had a strong understanding of alphabetic relationships. What actually precluded her from making that transition remains enigmatic. As I move into discussions of her first-grade year, I point out that part of the problem resided in the reading series that the school (and entire school district) had adopted as the central text for reading instruction. Laurie couldn't keep up with the expected progression laid out in this series, published by Houghton Mifflin, as inviting as the individual stories might have been for her as read-alouds or pretend-reading texts. She couldn't read the selections independently, and she fell further and further behind as her class moved through the series. Her confidence diminished as the text selections became impossible for her to process. However, I don't want to convey the story of Laurie's reading and writing in school as simply a history of being disabled by a system of institutional practices (e.g., published anthology texts, district mandates). There are other strands of her history that are important to write, involving sulky resistances in school and angry disruptions at home. As much as Laurie wanted to be a successful student, she encountered serious trouble that revolved around the material and emotional stresses of working-class family life. In kindergarten, Laurie was "acquired by" (see McDermott, 1996) a medical disorder that was to transform the shape of the year and impact her performances and identities throughout primary school.

Anger

My readings of Laurie's school experiences in kindergarten fall into two time periods: before and after she was medicated for her behavioral problems. Prior to Laurie's diagnosis, neither I nor Mrs. Thompson had noticed anything unusual about her behavior. Laurie sometimes expressed a sulky, adolescent-like resistance to an adult's request to try something a new way. She could on occasion be brassy or coy in her responses to peers. Nothing about her social or academic engagements, however, drew our eyes in a concerned manner to Laurie as she worked at the Writing Center, played in the house symbolic play area, and socialized with Nicholas and her other peers. However, in late winter, my fieldnotes suggested some changes in Laurie's behavior. Fieldnotes written in February describe Laurie as being out of sorts during symbolic play in the house area. Usually bubbly and confident in such settings, she seemed quiet and withdrawn. A seemingly minor peer conflict involving who would play the mom seemed to throw her off and interrupt her participation in the symbolic play.

In March of Laurie's kindergarten year, her teacher shared with me during one of our regular research meetings that Laurie had been diagnosed as having an attention deficit disorder. Because of her diagnosis, she had begun taking daily medication. The early ramifications of this change in Laurie's life were difficult to watch. Fieldnotes written after classroom observations in February reflect the ways in which there was a shift in Laurie's classroom behavior. Initially, she seemed more depressed and withdrawn; "in a funk" was the description used by her teacher. She complained of side effects. In March I was audiotaping children's "monster stories" as part of a classroom storytelling activity. I was surprised when Laurie balked at sharing her monster story. Typically, this would have been the kind of activity she loved. "I don't think I'm doing it," she said. When I pressed her to explain why, she responded, "I don't feel so good . . . 'cause them dumb pills make my stomach hurt." In the year-end review of Laurie's progress in kindergarten, we noted that she seemed to lose her voice after being diagnosed and medicated for ADD. Her earlier brassiness was more subdued. Thinking back on these changes now, it seems that one thing that shifted for Laurie was her feeling of power. The diagnosis changed her social relations in school in ways that extended beyond the side effects of the medication itself.

Angry feelings and actions were the impetus for Laurie's medical testing and diagnosis. As a kindergarten child, Laurie had developed some painful relations with adults at home. Amid the economic and child-care stresses faced by the adults, Laurie's needs and interests were sometimes lost. As the oldest daughter of a young mother who was struggling to make ends meet, work toward a college degree, and care for Laurie's two younger siblings, Laurie took on social roles that were conflictual for her. She saw herself at home as both caretaker and child. As she later shared with me in second grade, "I'm too old for my age." The role of caretaker or "mom" *and* child seemed both to empower her and complicate her life. Things were made more difficult by the fact that Laurie's relations with her younger sister were troubled. During my home visits with Laurie, stressful events often arose involving her younger sister. Jealousy over the attention I was paying to Laurie, for instance, could lead to attempts to disrupt our work. Laurie acted out amid these sibling and adult relationships in ways that became unmanageable in the context of an already stressful set of material circumstances. She flew into uncontrollable rages. Though I never saw such angry moments of acting out, I accept that such strong "outlaw emotions" (Jaggar, 1992) were a painful part of her relationships within her family.

Although I am able to understand reasons for Laurie to be angry, I do not see her angry feelings as something internal to her individually. Megan Boler (1999) argues that emotions are part of social relations and histories. As she writes, "Emotions are inseparable from actions and relations, from lived experience" (p. 2). Laurie's history differs significantly from my own childhood experiences in the ways in which anger surfaced in her family. Laurie's family members did not hold back anger or resentment. Strong emotions were outwardly expressed, including anger. Children knew well when adults were tired or annoyed, often because of the dual stresses of child care and employment. At times, Laurie took up similar angry stances in response to her younger sister, Brittany. For instance, during a home visit in second grade, Laurie's sister tried to climb on the kitchen table to get an object that Laurie saw as belonging to her little brother. In response, her entire body stiffening in anger, Laurie screamed, "GET OFF THERE!" During an earlier visit, I observed Laurie in symbolic play with Brittany. Laurie was enacting the role of the mother toward the "baby," her sister. Laurie said that she was going to have to smack Brittany. Later on, she held up a plastic golf club, moving toward Brittany as if to hit her, though never actually coming close enough to do so. Angry feelings and actions were expressed in ways that were sometimes uncomfortable for me as an observer. Having grown up in a rural southern setting, I was used to norms of restraint. If angry emotions were voiced in strong ways, they would not have been voiced, in my girlhood experiences, by women.

Though strong feelings were outwardly expressed among adult women in her family, Laurie's particular violences became connected to a medical disorder. Laurie is now considered a child with ADD; this has become part of her institutionalized history. As my research was coming to a close, a third-grade teacher informed me that Laurie was doing much better in school since her medication had been changed. However, I also view her ADD diagnosis as part of the situated relations she lived as a young girl. Though I accept the fact that she initially flunked the ADD test, I also believe that what has been marked is not her inability to focus, but her response to stressful material and emotional practices. Anger can be a powerful emotion, helping to uncover, as Boler argues, discomforts worth resisting. For little girls, however, anger can be risky, and violence can lead to subject positions linked to pathology (see Walkerdine, 1990, pp. 45–48).

It is of course possible for girls to be bad in school. Acting "bad" can be a means of gaining power for both girls and boys. Margaret Finders (1998) discusses how adolescent girls can be "bad" through open expressions of female desire and sexuality. Tammy Schwartz (1999) describes how middle school girls can defy institutional regulation through challenges to teachers. However, such overt resistances run the risk of being positioned as pathological within schools as institutions. In Schwartz's description of one girl's resistant behavior, aggression was met with suspension and the threat of psychiatric evaluation. Laurie's disruptive behaviors at home never surfaced in primary school. What did emerge as she moved into first grade were remnants of the tuning out that had occasionally surfaced in kindergarten—her stubborn refusal to try something new, or perhaps something academically challenging. In first grade, Laurie began to rummage in her desk or quietly chat with her peers during class lessons. Sulky, adolescent-like shrugs of her shoulders in response to requests from her kindergarten teacher went underground in first and second grade. Laurie's history in first and second grade was marked by her desires to be *good* for her teachers. As stories of classroom goodness emerge, however, so do stories of increasing academic distress. Maintaining a cherub-like schoolgirl demeanor, Laurie in first grade began living a dual existence as a model student who was learning how to fail.

LEARNING HOW TO BE A GOOD GIRL

In late summer, just before the start of second grade, Laurie talked with me about how she had learned to be good in school. In the early months of first grade, she told me, she hadn't been as good. She noticed how a boy in the classroom had received kudos for his good behavior, and she started to be good. She mentioned her Superstar award, which she had received in February for her exceptional behavior (she had first been chosen as Star of the Week and had later received this even more prestigious award). She shared with me how much she had loved her kindergarten and first-grade teachers, and how much she wanted to be good for her new second-grade teacher. We talked about how the coming year would be her last one at the primary school. She expressed her sadness at leaving the school. Overwhelmingly, she talked positively about her school and her teachers, showing a valuing of her goodness within school contexts. None of her academic struggles came out in Laurie's story, only her desire to continue to be good in school.

Laurie's desire to be good in school emerged in a context in which being "good" was a means of gaining power as a girl. In Laurie's primary school, a discourse of goodness and obedience was celebrated as a means of social regulation. From kindergarten onward, children learned to recite the school's ABC creed: Always Be Caring, Always Be Careful, Always Be Courteous, Always Be Cooperative—for a Beautiful Maple Dale and a Beautiful Child. Within this ideological system, children did become "good," winning rewards such as the coveted Star of the Month award that Laurie received in first grade. Even within what Dyson (1993) describes as peer social worlds, an ethic of moral goodness and obedience was enacted by some children, often by girls. Girls enacted their schoolgirl identities in part by voicing discourses of niceness and conformity to norms of practice. In a scene from Laurie's kindergarten year, for example, three girls enact such discourses as they work with a boy at a Centers table. All four children are coloring. The girls voice their displeasure at Gary's coloring job, socially positioning him as inept because he is not coloring neatly. At the same time, they construct themselves as successful students—doing the *real* schoolwork that will be required of first-graders:

> Gary moves to the Centers table where Brittany and Justina are coloring rainbows. They are soon joined by Nicole. At one point in their drawing and talk, Nicole asks a question (voiced to the whole group), and Gary responds. Nicole replies smugly, "I asked the *girls*." Earlier in this episode, the three girls working at this table had become quite coy, teasing Gary about his coloring. There was a big emphasis among the girls about the neatness of their colored rainbows. Brittany's rainbow, in particular, was extraordinary in its level of neatness. Several times, one of the three girls commented on the importance of neatness. At one point, one of the girls said something to Gary about having to learn to color (implying: color between the lines) before going to first grade. There was a sense I had of the three girls believing that they were doing real

schoolwork, and that they had to make sure Gary understood his shortcomings in this area. Gary retorted that *he* was going to draw the Power Rangers. He flipped over his rainbow ditto and drew some superhero figures. Justina responded by criticizing him for drawing a Power Ranger character that she claimed no longer existed. (Videotape and fieldnotes)

This episode of social sparring among children illustrates one means through which girls gain power in school. Though boys like Gary can gain power through voicing their resistance to the roles associated with being good, girls often seek power through being "nice, kind, and helpful" (Walkerdine, 1990, p. 76). Girls such as Justina, Nicole, and Brittany align themselves with the values they associate with real schoolwork and with their teachers, often women in primary school. Like my own attempt in second grade to produce a beautifully copied text, girls in Laurie's school embraced an ethic of female goodness.

As Walkerdine (1990) points out, girls can be both good *and* smart in school. Girls who both do well academically and are helpful and cooperative often have high classroom status:

> Good performance combined with docility and helpfulness presents a striking picture not unlike that expected of primary school teachers, who must possess capacities of nurturance to be "amplified," yet must reach the standard of attainment necessary for teacher training. Conversely, girls who are "nice, kind, and helpful" are more suited to facilitating nurturance. It is perhaps important, then, that many young girls do not understand high attainment and femininity as antithetical. Girls who "possess" both characteristics are highly validated. (p. 51)

In Laurie's first- and second-grade classrooms, there were girls who both met high academic standards and embraced an ethic of neatness and obedience. Laurie, however, was unable to be academically successful. She recognized that she was not meeting classroom expectations in subjects such as reading; she seemed to displace all her longings for moral goodness onto codes of good behavior. She sat stiffly upright in her chair when her first- or second-grade teachers asked which children were ready to be called on. She clasped her hands and placed them dutifully on her desk, waiting for her teacher's recognition. She wanted desperately to be good.

Interlaced with those schoolgirl efforts were Laurie's struggles as a reader in first grade. Reading emerged as one of the most problematic of school subjects for her as reading practices became defined in more constrained terms. As Laurie began to fall seriously behind in classroom reading and writing practices, I'm not sure what choices were available to her. She turned to peers for friendship, to boys for romantic interest, and to her teacher for positive acceptance, even as those valued relationships became increasingly complicated by her vulnerability as a student.

First-Grade Practices of Reading and Writing

The beginning of first grade was tough for many, if not most, of Laurie's classmates. The Mid-Atlantic late summer climate ensured that the weather was hot and muggy in late August and early September. Children were not used to all-day schooling, since kindergarten had only been a half-day. A scene from mid-September evokes the challenges faced by children and their teacher. As Laurie's teacher, Mrs. Rhodes, teaches a whole-class lesson on how to figure out new words they encounter in texts, Laurie and a neighbor put their heads on their desks. Jake (seated at another desk area) does the same. Another child closes his eyes wearily.

The rigor of academic work, particularly seatwork or lengthier periods of whole-class instruction, was new and tiring to many children. Some children also seemed unsure of the new academic tasks asked of them as first-graders. Shortly after this lesson, for instance, Laurie struggled with a "Spelling for Writing" worksheet that focused on the letters c and d. She copied the letters -og instead of writing the required d before them to form the word (dog) specified by the worksheet activity. This early difficulty settling into classroom routines involving more seatwork was familiar to Laurie's first-grade teacher, a seasoned teacher of young children. Yet somewhere along the way, most children in Laurie's classroom became successful participants in the discourse practices of this first-grade classroom. Children learned to read school texts, typically stories from their anthology and books in the classroom library. Children learned how to participate in class discussions, to do worksheets and morning papers, and to get rewards for good behavior.

Snapshots from a set of all-day observations done in early October evoke the kinds of literacy practices in which Laurie needed to participate as a new first-grader. After children have done their morning paper activities (e.g., a worksheet focusing on the color word brown), they go to the rug area for whole-class work. Part of this rugwork involves chorally reading a poem that incorporates number words. Children return to their seats for the beginning of language arts instruction. After some framing discussion of an anthology selection, Dear Zoo (by Rod Campbell), children read the selection chorally, most of them using their fingers to track printed text. Laurie does not follow with her finger, though she voices the parts of the text she already knows. Afterwards, children read the text once more, this time with a partner. They alternate reading pages. The anthology reading is followed by a whole-class lesson on rhyming words. Laurie's teacher works with the word from the story, *pet*, substituting its beginning letter to form words that rhyme with it (e.g., *wet*, *met*, *jet*). Laurie talks softly with her classmate Kurt during this discussion. This lesson is followed by a worksheet on which children have to do similar rhyming "word family" exercises. Another worksheet activity follows, in which children color pictures according to a key that connects beginning letter information to a certain color (e.g., an image with an *f* initial letter sound is colored yellow). After a break for lunch and recess, children come back to 10 minutes of Drop Everything and Read (DEAR) time. Laurie flips through some books without reading printed text. Later in this schoolday, as dismissal time approaches, children get their homework folders ready and hear a story, *Little Red Goldilocks*. Laurie can't find her homework folder, and her neighbor, Kurt, offers her a spare one.

While Laurie fully bought into a system of disciplinary behaviors and their rewards (e.g., Star of the Month or Superstar designations), she seemed lost and unsure amid the new academic practices required to be a successful first-grader. The literacy activities that were empowering for her in kindergarten, such as working at the Writing Center, were replaced with activities that brought out her vulnerabilities. She was able to tune out during a lesson on word families, focusing her energies on having a quiet chat with a boy seated next to her. She quickly lost the motivation to read on her own, since the anthology selections were too difficult for her. During DEAR time, her goal seemed to be one of getting kudos from her teacher for being good—for using her time wisely and quietly. Similarly, during whole-class discussions, she seemed eager to find the right answer for her teacher. Laurie's efforts to be good, however, didn't secure for her the forms of empowerment she had experienced in kindergarten.

An image of Laurie in May of her first-grade year stands in sharp contrast to images of her confidence as a kindergarten writer. Laurie and her classmates are participating in a writing activity in which they are to write stories about creatures they have created. Laurie copies her story from the writing done by an academically successful classmate, Brittany. The two pieces of writing end up being nearly identical in spelling and content:

BRITTANY'S CREATURE TEXT

My creature is
big an My creature
has big ers. it

has a pike meouth it es
appol and it ess treees.

(My creature is big and my creature has big ears. It has a pink
mouth and it eats apples and it eats trees.)

LAURIE'S CREATURE TEXT

My creature is
big na my creature
has big ers it
has a pik
meoth it es
ess thees

(My creature is big and my creature has big ears. It has a pink
mouth and it eats trees.)

One of the boys writing at the same desk area calls Laurie on her copying.
She bursts into tears at his accusation, vehemently denying that she is
copying. I step out of my role of observer and try to intervene, suggesting
to Laurie that we (those of us sitting at the desk grouping) really want
to hear about *her* ideas. She sobs uncontrollably.

By mid-year it had become apparent that Laurie was in serious trouble
academically. Her reading was far behind grade-level expectations; she
was still reading on a kindergarten level. Her math performances also
seemed shaky. Things were so fragile for Laurie that as early as January
Mrs. Rhodes began talking about the possibility of retention. What had
happened to Laurie—the young girl who in kindergarten had seemed so
strong and confident working at literacy centers?

On one level, things seemed fairly obvious. Laurie was unable in
first grade to build on her strengths from kindergarten. Though she had
made impressive gains in areas such as alphabetic knowledge, invented
spelling/writing, and reading highly predictable texts, Laurie needed
time to solidify her fluency and confidence as an emergent reader and
writer. In first grade, however, she participated in a literacy curriculum
that emphasized a linear path of development reflective of the school's
grade-level expectations. The school's literature anthology presented children's texts in a developmentally ordered sequence. Reading selections
were supplemented by phonics, writing, and spelling activities. The text
selections in the series were rich and inviting, and they were balanced
by ample work on word study and phonetic analysis. Laurie's teacher
understood that the reading selections presented did not match the needs
of struggling readers such as Laurie. However, Mrs. Rhodes seemed

committed to using the curriculum that the school had adopted and to supplementing it with worksheets and whole-class lessons that she devised herself. She was an experienced and committed first-grade teacher who worked hard to create what contemporary literacy educators argue is essential: a balanced curriculum that allows children to develop graphophonics skills and fluency (e.g., Osborn & Lehr, 1998; Snow et al., 1998). In Laurie's case, however, the particulars of the curriculum didn't come together for her. She was unable to put the pieces together when it came to the reading and writing practices expected of her.

Laurie's early difficulties and hesitancies snowballed into a major problem by mid-year, as she got further and further behind her more successful peers. In retrospect, what could have been an appropriate response to Laurie's difficulties was a literacy program that was individualized to her needs, along the lines of Reading Recovery (see Clay, 1993). In second grade, Laurie did enter her primary school's Chapter One reading program, with a focus on small-group instruction at children's individual reading levels. She seemed more confident in this supportive setting. However, the school could not afford a Reading Recovery program or its equivalent, and the Chapter One program for struggling first-grade readers was filled to capacity with children in more dire academic need than Laurie. Her early months of first grade were thus spent becoming an academically distressed student (see McDermott, 1996, for a comparable case study). Insecurities and resistances coalesced over these months. Relationally within her first-grade classroom, she was becoming an unsuccessful reader.

In January of first grade, I began working with Laurie as a tutor. Her teacher's warnings that Laurie was in danger of retention prompted my efforts to intervene—to help Laurie move through some of her difficulties with reading. During home visits after school, Laurie's mother or grandmother would graciously clear the kitchen table so Laurie and I could do literacy activities. I began collecting books that I thought more appropriate matches to Laurie's reading abilities, bringing these with me for each visit. I brought enticing writing paper and some "artists' crayons" I found at a children's toy store. Working closely with Laurie, I wanted to help her regain the confidence we had seen in kindergarten. Like her mother, grandmother, and first grade-teacher, I was also aware of the urgency of helping Laurie make progress as a young reader. The spring months of first grade would be crucial in determining whether she moved on to second grade with her peers. Because of her social maturity, I felt that retention would be exceedingly painful for Laurie. Her mother had mixed feelings about retention (she herself had repeated a grade), but she felt that one-on-one literacy work would be helpful to Laurie no matter what the final decision would be about second grade.

As I began to work with Laurie after school in her home, her kindergarten strengths and exuberance, visible the previous schoolyear, resurfaced. For example, in early March I had brought along with me a copy of a children's book, *Each Peach Pear Plum*, by Janet and Allan Ahlberg (1978), as well as some oversized paper for writing and drawing. Laurie and I started with some reading activities. I thought she would feel more supported if we read the text together before she read it on her own. I also felt that this book would be one that would grab her attention. It uses nursery rhymes in imaginative ways, involves an I Spy guessing game, has colorful illustrations that provide I Spy clues, and uses repetitive, rhyming text:

> Each peach pear plum
> I spy Tom Thumb (*Tom Thumb depicted in illustration*)
> Tom Thumb in the cupboard
> I spy Mother Hubbard (*Mother Hubbard depicted in illustration*)

These things would, I felt, help to motivate Laurie and support her reading—given her love of fantasy but also her need to read predictable and supportive texts. Even so, as she chimed in during our initial choral reading, Laurie seemed unsure of herself. She echoed even in this supportive context some of the mumbling and guessing tactics that had begun to characterize her reading in school. As I turned things over to her and flipped on my tape recorder, however, a different response emerged. Reading aloud to her beloved toy cat Snowflake, she read through the text with fluency and confidence that seemed a more accurate assessment of her strengths as an emergent reader. She was a reader, albeit one who needed a supportive social environment and text. As we turned to writing, the emergent literacies that were evident during kindergarten were visible. We decided that a good writing activity would be to describe Snowflake for her teacher, since Mrs. Rhodes had never met Snowflake. Laurie drew a picture of her toy cat and wrote a descriptive narrative about her (see illustration).

During these one-on-one sessions at home, Laurie seemed enthusiastic and confident as a reader and writer. However beneficial these sessions might have been for her, they did not seem to have a discernible impact on her evolving history in first grade. Her writing notebook remained sparse compared to those of her classmates, and her written compositions were largely formulaic "I like" sentences. Her reading fell below the norm

Snowflake the cat, by Laurie.

established in part by the sequence of children's texts in the school's adopted literature anthology. She ended the year being promoted to second grade, with the stipulation that her second-grade teacher would see how things went early in the year. A recommendation for Chapter One placement was made. Laurie was becoming a disabled reader within a context that defined reading according to grade-level expectations. She was starting to live between the contradictory social spaces of unnoticed fumblings in her desk, quiet talk with peers during whole-class lessons, and rewards for being good. Laurie resisted school by tuning out rather than through overt disruptions. She was never openly resistant in school.

At home, Laurie expressed her resistances differently. As she matured socially, she also developed more refined ways of butting heads with her mother and grandmother. She constantly challenged her mother, looking more to her grandmother as the authority figure. As her mother told me, Laurie had also in first grade begun to lie about things. Deceit had become one of the ways in which Laurie was maturing socially. Her resistance toward adults at home showed itself in ways that recalled her disruptive behavior in kindergarten. Laurie spent weekend and summer mornings at the laundromat where her grandmother worked during the day. Her medication was increased when Laurie got out of control, running from one end of the laundry to the other. Within a setting in which adults had work to get done, Laurie *was* out of control. She was also clearly in need—but in need of what? As a literacy educator, I saw Laurie struggling with school practices of reading, but I wondered how these were caught up in a girlhood history with painful contradictions—goodness and bad behavior, smiles and deceits, flirtations and peer rejections. I was becoming afraid for her.

In my efforts to advocate for Laurie, I tried to combine work on reading and writing with a nurturing relationship. We bonded around areas of common interest—activities such as writing and drawing and topics such as horses, magical places, and fairies and mythical creatures. One of the interests we shared in the spring was a love of gardens. Laurie was intensely interested in the flowering trees and plants that create a lush effect in the Mid-Atlantic springtime. I was at the time tending to a small courtyard garden. We read countless books on gardens, and Laurie composed stories about mythical gardens and their inhabitants. A story about a magic garden that emerged from one of our afternoon sessions in April reflects the increasingly subtle ways in which Laurie was learning how to live and give voice to seeming contradictions. In her fantasy stories, power and revenge were openly expressed. They were also an integral part of the beauty and goodness of her fictional worlds. Laurie's Magic Garden story gives voice to some things not as readily seen in the classroom. An openly passionate and revengeful narrator emerges—a good girl with her sword drawn. Was this her kindergarten creativity and brassiness gone underground, or perhaps a more mature form of identification with her mother's emotional vibrancy? Laurie's story points to a more intricate negotiation of girlhood fictions than a simple reading might suggest.

The Magic Garden

In her story, Laurie has created a row of flowers. The scene is a benevolent and tranquil one: The sky is blue, and brightly colored flowers are lined up. All the picture seems to require is a shining yellow sun. However, tragedy befalls one of the flowers, forecasting a delicate balance of good and evil, tranquility and violence, that becomes more evident as the story progresses. One of the flowers has been struck (by lightning?). Laurie's response, uttered in the voice of the narrator, is one of revenge; my voice, echoing a middle-class pedagogical discourse, reconstrues the tragic events into benevolent ones.* Whatever evil act has struck the flowers is linked to nourishment.

> LAURIE: I'm gonna draw some trees
>   here's a pond
>   put a little thing so it won't spill all over
>   there we go . . .
>   but something struck the light
> DEBORAH: ooooh, like lightening?
> LAURIE: it *breaked* one of the flowers!
> DEBORAH: oooooh
> LAURIE: I'm gonna kill (unclear word) who did it
>   and (unclear word) break the heart flower [*feigns crying*]
> DEBORAH: ooooh
> LAURIE: my masterpiece, I'm gonna kill it
> DEBORAH: your masterpiece
> LAURIE: my masterpiece
>   my stories are *ruined*
> DEBORAH: well sometimes you know what happens when it rains?
>   the lightening strikes and it rains
>   and the flowers get a lot of rain and water

---

*The following conventions are used in the transcription of Laurie's Magic Garden narrative. A space symbol (#) indicates a pause. An italicized word indicates emphasis. Italicized phrases or sentences indicate action or vocalizations, as opposed to speech.

LAURIE: oh!
> I'll make a lot of thunder then
> *Laurie makes sound effects of thunder/lightning*

DEBORAH: and it's so good for the flowers cause they can grow with the rain
> they love days like this [it's actually raining outside]
> so they're all getting, there's a lot of thunder

LAURIE: *sings to herself as she draws drops of rain*

DEBORAH: look at all that rain falling down

LAURIE: *it's goin on each flower*
> *one two three four five six, eight, eight flowers*

Laurie has appropriated one aspect of the interpretation lent to this emerging story, that destructive "striking" forces can be connected to rain, benevolent to the flowers in the magic garden. She adds big blue raindrops to her drawing, and these descend toward the row of garden flowers. However, the water itself becomes entwined in the tension between benevolence and destruction. The water in a pond adjacent to the row of flowers is blackened by devilish forces. Flowers that go near the "blood section" of the pond are killed.

DEBORAH: what's this? [*referring to a black spot near the top of the drawing*]

LAURIE: that's the haunted place

DEBORAH: the haunted place?

LAURIE: if any flower goes there, they'll be died
> they'll be died
> and they would join the dead (unclear word) . . .
> and it's that direction, don't go there

DEBORAH: don't go there

LAURIE: or they die
> there was [i.e., *used to be*] 13 [*flowers*]
> now the others disobeyed the ruler . . .
> I'm gonna make a speech balloon . . .
> it says "the others disobeyed and they're dead"
> "now don't ever # go # to the deepest # darkest # [unclear word]"

DEBORAH: don't ever go to the deepest darkest place?

LAURIE: no

DEBORAH: this is what the rose is saying?

LAURIE: don't go near the blood section . . .
> but an angel came down and picked up the flowers

DEBORAH: picked up these flowers?
LAURIE: uh hum
    and they stayed up there until they was ready to bloom
    angels picked up flowers until they're ready to bloom . . .

The plot thickens. As it progresses, Laurie's fictional story suggests increasingly complicated tensions between forces of good and evil, both of them powerful. An angel has given magical powers to the flowers; they alone are allowed to drink from another pond that has been made safe for them by a golden shield. However, the darkened water in the other pond remains a significant threat to the flowers, who are executed if they approach it. The rain, now benevolent in her appropriation of my earlier commentary on rain, drops on the flowers and fills the magic pond, but a single flower still experiences destruction when it fails to heed a warning about the dark pond.

DEBORAH: the black stuff is killing the water?
LAURIE: no
    everything is remained (unclear word) dark
    but each flower that drinks from this will die
    the devil's poison
    "don't touch that water or you'll die!"
    but I'm gonna give them water
    they're not gonna go on thirsty
    here's a little pond
    Laurie makes drinking/slurping sound effects
    they *marched* up there and got a drink
    but the devil didn't know
    they missed the uh big pond
    but that one [i.e., the big pond] is a magic pond
DEBORAH: this one is safe, it's magic
LAURIE: now if anybody touches it they'll kill 'em
    except the flowers
    watch out this is tricky now
    protected by a golden shield
DEBORAH: the pond's protected by a shield?
LAURIE: uh hum
    by the golden shield . . .
DEBORAH: but the flowers can drink from this water?
LAURIE: yes
    only the flowers can go through cause they have the best of
    powers . . .

DEBORAH: they have the best of powers?
LAURIE: um hum
   the angel gave it to 'em
   they're (unclear word) friends
   and they made rain come down to drip drop in the water
   so they'd get bigger and bigger
   this one's executed
DEBORAH: executed
LAURIE: that means "don't go near it" [*uttered with staccato rhythm*]
   "no no no!" [*high-pitched voice*]
   She writes: I LIKe the GrDeN bkis miGik gosar to the GrDe [I like
   the garden because magic goes to the garden]

Violence and goodness sit in complicated balance in Laurie's Magic
Garden story. Her story suggests a fictional world in which power, dark-
ness, and revenge live in close proximity to beauty and moral goodness.
A flower empowered by the forces of a good angel can still walk out into
a darkened, endangered world and face the resulting consequences. The
avoidance of violence adheres in the warning voiced by the narrator:
"Don't touch that water!" However, Laurie's story does not strike me as
an easy triumph of good forces over evil ones. The flowers in her story
are empowered by forces representing goodness and beauty (e.g., an
angel), vulnerable to danger, and capable of revenge. Early in the story,
one of the flowers is "broken" when struck. Later, the good flowers kill
some of their own ("they had to kill the other group") and then live with
the threat posed to them by their uneasy nearness to a pond darkened
by evil.

Laurie was in first grade learning how to live the contradictions of
little girlhood. She embraced discourses of femininity in the classroom,
even though those identities didn't allow much room for the anger and
resistance she expressed at home. She bought into an ethic of good behavior, perhaps aiming for an acceptance she couldn't get through her academic work. Cloaked as it was by her exceptional classroom behavior,
Laurie's academic distress could go unnoticed from day to day. She increasingly played out an imagined space for herself—mumbling along
to show her participation, looking for just the right moment to perk up
and be a good listener. If she bought into a classroom ethic of niceness,
her narrated stories suggest a more nuanced reading of goodness. Anger
and resistance were part of her responses to the practices around her,
along with her struggles for power. As a first-grader, however, Laurie
was learning to negotiate more nuanced roles for herself within these
complicated realities. She was learning deceit at home and the value of

being quiet at school. Such is the world of girlhood, or so I have known it: a subtle dance between academic practices, concealed power, and the careful display of feeling. However, Laurie's charting of a biographical course between such relations may well differ from my own. Whereas I immersed myself in symbolic worlds in school, increasingly the worlds of literary texts, Laurie had not formed those kinds of attachments to reading practices. Literacy remained problematic for Laurie, as powerful and poetic her narrated stories might have been.

POWERFUL STORIES OF GIRLHOOD

Reflecting on Carolyn Steedman's (1982) study of second-grade girls' writing, Jane Miller (1996) argues that literacy can afford girls a means of reinventing gendered subject positions. As Miller writes:

> Little girls, in their play, are apt to burlesque, with manic and bustling energy, those endless tasks: washing, cooking, shopping, cleaning, smacking, rocking. Their longing for miniature ironing boards and dolls in prams may astonish their modern mothers. And their simultaneous desire for fairy dresses with wings and a make-up kit will scarcely redress the balance. Yet reading and writing may work as a way for them to make sense of those contradictions. Literacy provides them with stories of princesses and beggar maids, and of bad girls as well as good ones. These become something more, I think, than a comfort or an escape. Literacy becomes a mode of living femininity as more than just "negative capability." It offers scope for imagining multiplicity and change, and for resisting, as well as yielding to, the seductions of the domestic and the feminine. (p. 210)

Such was the case in my own girlhood history, as I looked to literary texts for stories that I could juxtapose with lived realities. Laurie also engaged responsively with the literary texts she encountered. However, the stories having the most power and authority for her were ones connected to her mother's romances and desires for better material living conditions. A story of love, happiness, and material comfort became prominent in Laurie's second-grade year in school. Dreams of a new daddy made their way into Laurie's writing and helped her gain confidence in school. Her second-grade Writer's Notebook is especially revealing of the power of those attachments and desires. It also suggests a disturbing pattern of dissonance that was to emerge between Laurie's girlhood dreams for love and domestic happiness and her lived realities. If Miller's hopeful arguments are to hold true for girls such as Laurie, then a question for educators becomes: How do we help girls shape those kinds of critical engagements with literacy practices? Laurie's history in second grade reveals how complicated a response to this question can be, even for educators seeking social justice for poor and working-class girls.

Second-Grade Practices of Reading

Laurie began second grade on shaky ground. However, then in my third year of observing and working instructionally with Laurie, I was hopeful that she would regain some of the academic confidence I had observed in kindergarten and later in tutoring sessions. Her second-grade teacher had become over the years a local expert on language arts pedagogies. Mrs. Williams had completed a master's degree in literacy education and had attended workshops led by prominent language arts educators. She implemented Writing and Reading Workshops in which children worked at their independent levels and received supportive guidance. She had amassed over the years an extensive children's literature collection that she used instead of the school's adopted anthology series. However, she strove for a balance between these so-called whole-language pedagogies and ones that called for explicit teaching of genre, phonics, and spelling patterns. The classroom had a word wall that displayed spelling patterns, and children worked regularly on letter chunking—exploring parts of words having recurrent spelling patterns. Importantly for Laurie, literacy instruction was individualized. Children chose books that they could read independently during Reading Workshop. They wrote about topics of personal interest in Writing Workshop. This seemed like a hopeful school setting for a young girl struggling with academic expectations that she had not been able to meet.

Snapshot images from practices enacted in this classroom in early September illustrate what Laurie encountered as a new second-grader. Early in the morning, children write for 10 minutes in their Writer's Notebooks. Mrs. Williams writes along with the children. She shares with me later that she wants to establish a time for writing—a writing disposition—even if not all children compose something during the 10 minutes. Laurie sits quietly, not yet writing. Next, children do choral reading from poetry anthologies—notebooks with photocopied poems chosen by Mrs. Williams. Laurie has difficulty matching her pointing finger to the words being chorally read, though she attempts to participate. Ten minutes later, Mrs. Williams leads the class in some focused work on spelling and letter chunking. Children write their best guesses for the spelling of words called out by Mrs. Williams, words such as *neat*. Afterwards, children work on an activity patterned after the book *A House Is a House for Me*. They make their own "books" using the repetitive phrasing from the text and substituting different kinds of houses and their inhabitants (e.g., a *web* is a house for a *spider*). Library time follows, and all leave the classroom. Upon returning, children participate in 30 minutes of independent and paired reading. Laurie chooses a book that I know she cannot read, and I urge her to find something she can read. "I know where there are some books I can read," she says, going over to a basket where there are some Sunshine (beginning reader) books. She reads one of the Sunshine books successfully.

After a break for lunch, followed by recess and math, Mrs. Williams reads the book *Up Goes the Skyscraper* and discusses it with the children. The book and the earlier bookmaking project are tied to a theme unit on communities and buildings. The book shows different phases of a construction project. Afterwards, children bring to the group rug area Lego buildings they had previously constructed, and they collectively form a "community" of buildings. Toward the end of the day, children participate in a Writing Workshop. Mrs. Williams encourages children to return to their Writer's Notebooks to retrieve topics and ideas for writing. Children are given a writing folder with blank sheets of lined paper and a separate sheet for brainstorming topics. Each child has written down at least several possible topics. Brittany, Laurie's immediate neighbor, composes a lengthy piece, as do a number of children in the classroom. Many of the children were first-grade students of Mrs. Williams the previous year, since she has "looped" to second grade. They are therefore familiar with Mrs. Williams's Writing Workshop routines and set to work quickly. Laurie struggles initially with her piece but sticks with it. Her written composition on this mid-September day in second grade utilizes a supportive "I like" frame:

> I LKE To Rood a bok be
> casy iT is Funniy
>
> (I like to read a book because it is funny.)

Laurie continued to write "I like" compositions throughout the early months of second grade and to read simple, predictable texts during Reading Workshop. In October, she was also admitted into the school's Chapter One program for small-group reading instruction. Around that same time she began to receive individual tutoring from a preservice teacher education student doing a field placement at her school. Given the individualized focus of the writing curriculum in Mrs. Williams's classroom and the supportive reading contexts in which Laurie participated, she was able to read and write in ways that were comfortable for her. Yet she struggled and sometimes tuned out during other activities. My notes from a classroom visit in October suggest that during a whole-class reading of poetry from the children's poetry notebooks, Laurie seemed disconnected. At times like this, she fumbled in her desk or seemed to stare into space. Laurie also occasionally spoke of the academic vulnerabilities she continued to experience. During a partner-reading activity in which she read *City Mouse, Country Mouse* with an academically stronger peer, Laurie pointed to the final pages of the book and said, "I can't wait 'till we get to the end of here." Her reading was slow and labored, and her reading partner, Yvonne, stepped in frequently to provide support.

In November, something changed for Laurie. Whereas throughout the early fall she had frequently seemed disconnected from whole-class lessons, in late fall she began to express excitement about school. Observational notes from a classroom visit in mid-November show Laurie highly engaged in a discussion about regrouping and subtraction. Laurie had just returned from some tutoring work in reading and walked in part way through a math activity involving cubes. Children worked with sets of cubes at their desks and also checked their work against a model that Mrs. Williams constructed once children had voiced their solutions. Laurie became immediately involved in the activity of subtracting cubes from her set. She seemed confident and sure of herself. After completing with cubes the problem of taking away 10 from 18, she wrote the number *8* quickly, saying excitedly, "I got it, eight!" Mrs. Williams praised her attentiveness and involvement. Laurie crossed her legs smugly. In December, close to the winter holiday season, Laurie returned from her Chapter One session with glitter on her cheeks. She seemed bubbly, gleeful.

Laurie's excitement in school in late fall and winter may have been connected to her happiness about a new father in her life. In late fall she began to think she would have the father she so badly wanted, as there had been talk of engagement and marriage for her mother. In January Laurie shared with me during a classroom visit that she was getting a new daddy. However, in February she commented as I entered the classroom early in the morning, "My daddy, he's not coming back." Changes in this important relationship may have contributed to the variability in Laurie's responses to academic activities. On some occasions, she seemed excited and engaged; on others, detached and distant. By early spring Mrs. Williams was expressing serious concerns about Laurie. She was still reading at a kindergarten level in second grade. Observational notes from mid-April show Laurie rummaging in her desk during a choral reading, clearly disengaged from the activity. Mrs. Williams shared with me in late April that Laurie was one of only two children whom no one had chosen for a seating partner when children had been allowed to choose their seating arrangements. We suspected that this was due to Laurie's copying. We discussed the serious possibility that Laurie would not make it in third grade and might need to be retained.

The relationships and events that shaped Laurie's home life in second grade help to shed light on her participation in reading practices in school. Her history as a young reader is most richly understood in terms of this dual lens. While Laurie was learning to juggle the demands of second-grade academic expectations, she was dealing with some of the most powerful events in her girlhood thus far. The presence of a longed-for daddy changed the landscape of her life at home, but it also added some new complications. Laurie's problematic relations with adults at home remained part of her evolving schoolgirl history, even as she reveled in romantic dreams. She inserted herself into a story of love, material comforts, and family happiness. The more subtle dimensions of that story were not things she voiced or perhaps even acknowledged. In second grade, Laurie looked for domestic and romantic bliss. She wrote these into powerful stories of girlhood in her Writer's Notebook, as she explored new fictions of romance for herself.

Someday My Prince Will Come

Drawing on a friend's recounting of a song lyric ("Someday my prince will come . . . "), Walkerdine (1990) writes of the ways in which little girls are prepared for femininity by certain textual devices. Romantic stories and fairy tales typically end with girls inserted happily into an idealized marriage. Teen magazines and media images portray what is needed for "getting and keeping a man" (p. 90). Laurie strongly embraced such textual fictions about romance and marriage. Talk of a possible marriage for her mother led Laurie to construct a fantasy world in which this new and exciting man in her life would transform things, leading to a fairy tale, happily-ever-after ending. A story written by Laurie in December of second grade reflects such moral fictions. In the story, Laurie creates a fantasy scenario in which she is the flower girl at her mother's wedding and bearer of the diamond ring—a symbol of her new daddy's love and material wealth. The feelings and values expressed in this written text evoke the textual devices described by Walkerdine. After a beautiful wedding ceremony, all go home to live happily together.

> My mom had a wedding. I was the flower girl. My mom was so happy to see me when I got to [go] up at the ceremony. My mom gave me a case. I had the diamond ring. Mark got the ring on my

mom's hand and we all had white cake together. It was good and we went home and had dinner. It was good too. We was happy.

Laurie's life was transformed in second grade by the appearance of this new man in her mother's life. She was painfully aware that her real father would not be there for her. I think she saw her mother's relationship as a fairy tale with two sides to it. This new adult man would bring her mother emotional and material happiness. At the same time, he would bring happiness and love to the entire family, especially to Laurie. Laurie construed him as the daddy for whom she had longed. In the mornings she got up and made him breakfast. She looked forward to getting gifts of money when he returned from a business-related trip. She considered him "personal" (meaning having a nice personality) and well off. This new relationship seemed to empower Laurie, providing her with a happy storyline that included her in various roles—kitchen helper, flower girl, and daughter. Though the romance that for Laurie included *her* had a complicated trajectory, it was a focal point of her life in second grade. She wrote this fantasy into her Writing Workshop stories, and she lived its fictions in loving gazes toward the man she hoped would be her prince.

Such is the power of stories, as they assume moral weight and influence in the context of our histories. For Laurie, a romantic fiction that cast her as the recipient of the loving attention of a longed-for daddy became an integral thread in her personal history in second grade. Such cultural storylines achieve their power through how they are lived within histories of relations with others. They help shape our subjectivities because of their connections to others whom we value and love. As Bronwyn Davies (1993) writes:

> We not only read and write stories but we also live stories. Who we take ourselves to be at any one point in time depends on the available storylines we have to make sense out of the ebb and flow of being-in-the-world along with the legitimacy and status accorded to those storylines by the others with whom we make up our lives at any one point in time. (p. 41)

Laurie embraced a fairy tale romance and its promise of happiness as a strong bond of connection with her mother. Within her mother's history of romance, Laurie could insert herself in the roles accorded to little girls. She could be the happy flower girl, wearing a lovely dress and carrying the diamond ring. This satisfied Laurie's need to have an adult man who loved her. Given her descriptions of herself in relation to boys, this kind of fantasy also projected ahead to Laurie's more mature romantic dreams. For surely the kind of man whom she viewed as personable and generous would someday be her very own kind of romantic prince.

On our way home from a trip to Borders Bookstore in second grade, Laurie and I began to discuss the subject of her current boyfriend. I asked who her boyfriend was, and she told me that she still considered Steven (from first grade) her boyfriend. The two were no longer in the same classroom, but they saw each other on the playground and at lunch. My notes written about our dialogue suggest changes in the ways in which Laurie was narrating herself in romantic stories. She conveyed a sense of the intricate dance and struggles for power that romance in second grade involves:

> I asked her why Steven was her boyfriend, what made him special for her so that he would be her boyfriend. She said that he was nice to her. She told me the story of how last year Steven, who was then with a boy whom Laurie identified as his cousin, tried to kiss her. Laurie responded with a slap, though in her telling of things she was careful to convey the *kind* of slap it was. She emphasized that this was just a "little slap." She had begun by caressing Steven's face (she demonstrated with a lingering caress of her own face), but this had turned into a slap. I asked her what Steven did in response, and she said that his eyes opened wide. I asked Laurie if this was a real or imaginary story, since we had only that afternoon been looking at picture-books that we identified as imaginary tales. She insisted that it was real. (Fieldnotes)

As my discussion with Laurie went on, she continued by describing herself as desirable but also reticent to express her passions. In one part of these stories constructed about Steven, Laurie said that a girl in Steven's second-grade classroom had been trying to steal him away from her. In Laurie's telling of things, the other girl was presented as actively trying to woo Steven, with Steven maintaining eyes only for Laurie. Another thread of this discussion led Laurie to comment that boys hit girls but that girls didn't hit boys. Laurie's self-narration about girls withdrawing from boys' advances and aggressions, however, ignores the fact that, in her fictional story, it was she who hit Steven.

Practices of reading were interwoven with these important changes in Laurie's life and her understanding of herself. In spite of all the responsibilities being juggled—child care, working six days a week, domestic housework, and a new relationship—Laurie's mother read with her each night. Laurie's mother worked hard so that her daughter's history in school could be different from her own. As a student, Laurie's mother had struggled with reading. She, too, had been stronger in mathematics. Laurie and her mother read up to two books each evening from the book-in-a-bag selections sent home with Laurie. Still, reading practices were caught up in the difficult ways in which Laurie related to adults who were managing too many pieces. With a new member of the household present, Laurie looked for ways to gain power and control among three adults. She was increasingly resistant to adults, even as she identified with her mother.

When we think of literacy practices in terms of children's appropriation of linguistic texts, as discourses are sometimes viewed, we miss something crucial. Behind those discourses are attachments with concrete, speaking individuals. I think Laurie looked to me and other teachers for identity and belonging, as she wanted to engage in the practices that we valued. However, she must have found herself caught between competing identities at home and at school. To help Laurie figure out her place within them might have been an appropriate starting point for critical action. Her words, her stories, her readings of things—these would have been crucial. In second grade, Laurie created literary texts that could have been such a critical location. She appropriated the task of keeping a Writer's Notebook into an increasingly detailed fantasy about The Good Life. Caught up in a pedagogy of transparent meanings and mastery of forms, these girlhood fictions stood as unquestioned artifacts. I wish now that these written compositions could have become locations for a stronger activist agenda—for pushing Laurie to think about what she was writing, and why. There were tensions in her writing, gaps. With the wisdom that hindsight provides, I can now see these as points for critical analysis, with Laurie and her peers. That kind of analysis certainly would have engaged Laurie's intellect, and maybe even her desire for power.

WRITING FICTIONS OF GIRLHOOD

In her second-grade Writer's Notebook, Laurie created fantasies reflecting her desire for social acceptance and power. She projected a happy family life in which she was a key player. She fantasized that she was the owner of a brilliant horse that took her for rides every bit as thrilling as those experienced by the fictional Bellerophon atop his flying horse, Pegasus. And in the latter half of her second-grade year, Laurie began to explore a topic that entailed conflict for her: her friendships with other children in the classroom. Sometimes her school friends were nice to her, accepting and embracing her in the classroom and on the playground; at other times, they were less so. While Laurie wrote fantasies in which she was a valued and accepted friend, threaded into these were also reflections on the complexity of school relations for an academically vulnerable girl.

Her second-grade compositions initially drew on formulaic genres, such as the "I like . . . " textual frame, that require only that the young writer fill in the blank. Through the early fall, Laurie composed many pieces such as an early "I like" entry about horses and unicorns:

WRITER'S NOTEBOOK ENTRY (9/26)

I Like To Rida my horse
be casa it is Fun to rida . . .
And I like unicorns to

(I like to ride my horse because it is fun to ride. And I like unicorns too.)

Such formulaic compositions as these put Laurie far behind her second-grade classmates, many of whom were writing lengthy personal narratives at the beginning of the year. However, by late fall and early winter Laurie had shifted to narrative writing, having appropriated the genres valued in Writing Workshop. Many of Laurie's classmates, particularly girls, wrote about their pets and family events and their classroom friendships. Laurie drew on these shared peer social worlds as she appropriated narrative forms for writing during Workshop time (see Dyson, 1993). She began to attempt writing personal stories of greater length and complexity. Her experiences became grounds for writing descriptions that recalled the artistic self-images she asserted as early as kindergarten. She wrote in a poetic fashion about events as simple as examining a seashell.

WRITER'S NOTEBOOK ENTRY (1/10)

Wen I wat to the bech I fond a smoth shell
it was black white LIke a zebra
it was so betutfll
I put it in my Pokit and I tot the shell home
and thn I tot the shell
and I put the shell en my crab box so they cn have a home to lev in
the 3 crabs Liket the shell
they put there hads in

(When I went to the beach I found a smooth shell. It was black [and] white like a zebra. It was so beautiful. I put it in my pocket and I took the shell home. And then I took the shell and I put the shell in my crab box so they can have a home to live in. The three crabs liked the shell. They put their heads in.)

The Writing Workshop as a framework for teaching writing has been critiqued for being uncritically focused on young writers' development of an authorial voice, typically through the instructional emphasis placed on narrative. Advocates of genre instruction have argued that young writers, especially those from non-middle-class communities, need explicit instruction in the genres providing access to middle-class linguistic power structures (see Cope & Kalantzis, 1993; Freedman & Medway, 1994; Reid, 1987). Though Laurie might have benefited from explicit discussions about text forms, the open-ended structure of Workshop and her Writer's Notebook seemed to help her gain confidence. Her compositions became longer and more complex. She gained more control over spelling patterns. At the same time, Laurie's writings sometimes reflected an eery dissonance between her fantasies and the realities of her material experience. She wrote about Norman Rockwell–like scenes of family life and adventures with an imaginary horse. These were images of what Laurie wanted for herself. In that sense, writing in second grade created a safe space for exploration and risk taking, much like at the kindergarten Writing Center. Even riskier were the realities of Laurie's life. Within a writing curriculum emphasizing developmental progressions and personal voice, the tensions and contradictions she lived and ultimately wrote into her stories were only obliquely recognized.

Laurie's Writer's Notebook entries often dealt with three discernible topics. Threaded throughout her Notebook were stories about family events and relationships—ones in which she participates in warm, happy scenarios. Laurie's Flower Girl narrative, discussed earlier, is one such example of these important fictions of girlhood. Another is a story written after the Christmas holidays. Many of her classmates composed holiday narratives that described getting a Christmas tree and decorating it, and getting presents on Christmas morning (virtually all the children in Laurie's school celebrated this Christian holiday). Laurie's entry in early January related this theme to storylines of happy family life during the holiday season.

WRITER'S NOTEBOOK ENTRY (1/2)

On cresms day i got up oly that day
I hrd the fiyr popwg the popcorn
i wok my mo and my momomomo to and my str and bruthr to
we opnd the presns
i wes hapy wen i sall the now hose
i wes happy to see it wis the thing that I owe wtd
a beg hose

we all had a grat time to gathr
we eat the pop con to gethr

(On Christmas day I got up early that day. I heard the fire popping the popcorn. I woke my mom and my mom-mom too and
my sister and brother too. We opened the presents. I was happy
when I saw the new horse. I was happy to see it was the thing I
always wanted: a big horse. We all had a great time together. We
ate the popcorn together.)

This story exemplifies a writing technique that Laurie employed
throughout her Notebook: She took events with some grounding in her
lived experiences and rewrote them, casting herself and others in scenarios
that were partly fictional. In this Christmas story, Laurie and her family
woke up to the sounds of popcorn popping. Her family members participated in the opening of presents, and Laurie received the present of her
dreams. She and others were happy together as a family.

Laurie's fantasies about a social world characterized by intimacy and
happiness began in mid-year to be threaded into a series of stories about
horses. Perhaps drawing on the literary storylines about relations between
girls and their horses, such as in the *Misty of Chincoteague* or *My Little
Pony* books, Laurie began to construct an elaborate set of fictions about
her horse. In her stories, Laurie regularly visited her grandparents' farm,
where her horse resided. Laurie depicted herself astride the gorgeous
spotted horse as it rode "like the wind" and jumped as if it were "almost
flying" in the air.

WRITER'S NOTEBOOK ENTRY (1/30)

My horse is beyuty Foll to me and my stre and brathr to
She can rid Like the wend
whene She jups it looks Like she is omost fliing
hr cellrs are brown and black
Ohmost Like a Downmasn if it was black and white
avr wekand I go to my moomoms and pupup to spnd [final word
unclear]

(My horse is beautiful to me and my sister and brother too. She
can ride like the wind. When she jumps it looks like she is almost
flying. Her colors are brown and black, almost like a Dalmatian if
it was black and white. Every weekend I go to mom-moms and
pop-pops to spend [final word unclear].)

A Writer's Notebook entry dated January 15 is the initial reference
to these fictions, in which Laurie became a girl who spent afternoons and

weekends at the farm. In that first entry, Laurie wrote, "I got a horse at the frme it is beyoytefull." (I got a horse at the farm. It is beautiful.) She also wrote that "a duk was bone I got to kep the duk." (A duck was born. I got to keep the duck.) In a later entry, she described how she went apple picking and then made a pie. Her fictional visits to the farm were full of healthful adventures in which she was the lucky visiting grand-daughter—riding her horse, picking ripe apples, enjoying the shared activity of cooking apple pie, and heading back home in the evening hours.

WRITER'S NOTEBOOK ENTRY (2/12)

I Like to go to my momom and my pups frm
my momomo and pupup has a aplle ochrd
evy day wehn I go thr I go to the aplle orchd
and I take my hyg bskit and I pik the ripst redest apelles in the apelle orchd
I pek 100 aplles in the aplle orchrd to mak a piy
a aplle piy
when we mad aplle piy I mad a piy to
then it is tim to go hom
10:00

(I like to go to my mom-mom and my pops' farm. My mom-mom and pop-pop has an apple orchard. Everyday when I go there I go to the apple orchard, and I take my huge basket and I pick the rip-est reddest apples in the apple orchard. I pick 100 apples in the apple orchard to make a pie, an apple pie. When we made apple pie I made a pie too. Then it is time to go home. 10:00.)

As late as April, Laurie composed a descriptive piece in which she compared her horse to a unicorn.

WRITER'S NOTEBOOK ENTRY (4/8)

my horse is the butfl horse you ever sesn
She is black and whie Like a domshin
She ken run Like wind and She kn jupe in the scay
and Shey loks Lake a unicorn

(My horse is the [most] beautiful horse you ever seen. She is black and white like a Dalmatian. She can run like wind and she can jump in the sky and she looks like a unicorn.)

These were important fictions for Laurie. She could be the girl riding a stunning horse, and the girl picking apples and making pie alongside loving family members. These are fictions to which so many girls aspire— images of power and freedom along with the warmth of intimacy. Laurie appropriated these images of girlhood using the spaces of her Writer's Notebook to imagine herself living in different material realities.

Laurie also wrote about friendship. As things stood, she sometimes had difficulty negotiating friendships within school practices. Her academic neediness created an uncomfortable set of dynamics, in which she was sometimes viewed negatively. Laurie's stories of friendship therefore often take her outside the classroom and onto the playground, where she could be a popular girl. Laurie wrote about how she and her peer group liked to play "Dogs" outside after lunch—to pretend they were dogs and chase one another around the playground. An entry in mid-December, for instance, narrated Laurie's feelings about a girl in the classroom whom she hoped would be her friend.

WRITER'S NOTEBOOK ENTRY (12/18)

I Like My frend Brittany and My frend to
We Play dogs and chas Tim
then Tim chas us
Im the fasts dog
We not run Tim
No bute can git us
We Play It avury day

(I like my friend Brittany and my friend too. We play dogs and chase Tim. Then Tim chases us. I'm the fastest dog. We [out?] run Tim. Nobody can get us. We play it every day.)

While Laurie wrote about friendships and their importance to her, she also wrote about complications and conflicts she experienced with friends. In the spring, she wrote a series of reflections that explored an ambiguity that her friendships could entail. Sometimes she felt wanted and liked by her friends, other times less so. Her entry about her "two best friends" is an example of how she began late in the year to introduce this more complex topic into her Notebook writings.

WRITER'S NOTEBOOK ENTRY (3/27)

My 2 best friends.
Sumtimes thay are nisc to me.

and sume times they are mene to my
but now one ev my friends are being nics to me.

(My Two Best Friends. Sometimes they are nice to me. And sometimes they are mean to me. But now one of my friends is being
nice to me.)

In a piece that appeared soon after, in the heart of spring weather
and therefore playground time, Laurie described her relationships within
this peer group as "useful" because she was the "always the slow one."
Laurie was describing her speed on the playground. However, her narrative might be read as reflective of her stance within a peer group. She is
accepted, but only because she is not threatening to those in power. In a
later piece of writing (May 12), Laurie described Erika as "the leader"
and Brittany as "fastest" relative to Laurie, self-depicted in the entry
below as the "slow one."

WRITER'S NOTEBOOK ENTRY (4/9)

My frinds
I like my friends. erika and Brittany
Sume times thy Like me and sume Times thy dot Like me.
but erika is bying nise to me
I think Brittany Likes me but I No that [it's] becuse she ses [I'm]
slowe
We ohws play dogs
I'm ohws The sloe oen
but I no that it is yousfll to the teme because I No it.
and my teme
the End

(My Friends. I like my friends, Erika and Brittany. Sometimes they
like me and sometimes they don't like me. But Erica is being nice
to me. I think Brittany likes me but I know that it's because she
says I'm slow. We always play dogs. I'm always the slow one but
I know that it is useful to the team because I know it. And my
team. The end.)

What Laurie seemed to want in school was a sense of belonging that
was made more difficult by her academic vulnerabilities. Brittany and
Erika were academically strong and "good" behaviorally. They were
viewed as model students. Laurie strove for social acceptance within this
peer group. However, friendships could shift and were connected to

issues of power. Who was fastest (or smartest?) and who assumed leadership—these were important aspects of friendships in second grade. Amid those peer relations, Laurie was valued and "useful" in part because of her slowness within the group.

The later entries in Laurie's Writer's Notebook present a portrait of a young girl struggling with who she could be. Laurie took substantial risks in writing about her vulnerabilities as well as her desires. Though insecure about her academic problems, Laurie was willing to explore multiplicity in her writings. She shaped into storied form some powerful fantasies that cast her in changing roles. Viewed through a more explicitly political lens, however, school writing practices did not accord Laurie the support she needed for exploring different ways of living femininity. There was a troubling dissonance between her fictions of life on the farm, the material realities of her home and neighborhood, and her desire for friends and family to love and accept her. The contradictions between her fantasies and her material realities created points of tension. Maybe those gaps would have been a place to help Laurie and other girls in her classroom talk and write about the powerful meanings and practices shaping their lives. Maybe reading practices could have been brought into that more critical teaching agenda.

Laurie's strong and enduring relationship to writing became much shakier after second grade. As Laurie entered third grade, in a school system that emphasized traditional academic skills in the intermediate grades, school literacy practices became increasingly elusive for her. She struggled in school, with the exception of time spent in a supportive Chapter One reading program. At the time that I was concluding the research study involving Laurie, preparing for a move to another region of the country, there was further talk of retention. Some crucial opportunity for empowering education had been lost, I concluded, though I did not know how to change a school system so that Laurie could become the girl she longed to be in school.

SCHOOLING FOR WORKING-CLASS GIRLS

Close to the end of my 3-year study of the lives of working-class children, Laurie and I went on the trip to Borders Bookstore that I have described. We luxuriated in the fun of spending the afternoon together on a cold winter's day—of sipping hot chocolate and coffee in the café and going shopping. Laurie had received a $5 gift certificate for filling up a Borders Young Readers Club card with stickers for books she had read. We had made the trip to Borders to reap the benefits of her hard work over the summer and fall. When we actually tried to find a book that would suit her tastes and reading abilities, however, Laurie and I encountered some of the conflict that sometimes cropped up in the classroom. She only had $5 to spend, so her options were limited. I had in mind a paperback with some text in it, something she could *read*. When I nudged her toward the picture book section (where I knew we could find some easy reading books in her price range), she seemed restless and distracted, anxious to find something quickly. As I soon discovered, she had something different in mind than I did. It was getting close to Valentine's Day, and there was a special display of Valentine's books, cards, and games. There, something special caught her eye: a pop-up game book with winged doll figures, something like cardboard Barbie dolls with wings. Since I had been working with Laurie on reading and trying to shape a desire for reading books, I cajoled her out of the game book. My job was a little easier since the doll book was out of her price range anyway. We finally reached a compromise. Laurie located in this same display area a miniature Valentine's book that cost $4.99. It was basically an alphabet book, with different Valentine's messages on each page. At the end was an envelope for the young reader to send a message to someone.

Thrilled with the whole afternoon and Laurie's lucky find (and perhaps a little relieved to have found something within her price range and pleasing to both of us), we made our way back to the small, off-white house where Laurie lived. As we entered, the life she lived at home hit me—the bustle of two younger children playing in the house, the constant business of adult women tending to household tasks such as folding clothes. Laurie's sister was crying; her even younger brother, now a rambunctious preschooler, was running about the house waving a toy gun and playing Batman. Laurie began cutting one of the pages from the Valentine ABC book and stuffing it in the envelope attached to the back. She asked what my initials were, writing *M.* (for *Ms.*) before *D.H.* to make what I soon realized was a Valentine's message addressed to me. She handed me the envelope, and I thanked her profusely as I made my way out the door. As I was leaving, she said, "I love you." I said, "I love you, too."

This moment of social negotiation between adult woman and young girl encapsulates some of the complexities of living and learning between social classes. There we were, each living out the practices and values we had come to appreciate and desire. The minor conflict that did occur was easily negotiated, as I nudged Laurie toward what I wanted her to do. She bought into a form of literacy that met me halfway at least. Our relationship, which by that time was one of mutual caring and acceptance, helped to make such movement between practices possible. Though we were living our lives in different class settings, we were in this moment of teaching and learning able to move between and across those disparate locations. Such movement in classrooms is possible, too, but it requires a kind of commitment and knowledge that is getting hard to achieve amid the stresses of teaching in contemporary educational contexts. With classes that are too large to manage and increasingly stiff curriculum mandates, it has become difficult for teachers to come to know children with the kind of depth that engenders successful change. A response that is seemingly indicative of a lag in "development" may be, when we look more deeply, only one manifestation of a complicated web of class-specific relations. Children's histories and agencies are so readily reduced to simplistic theories and equally simplistic solutions. The paths to creating negotiated movements between cultures and classes are, however, never simple—never reducible to a single method of teaching or theory of learning. Such moments of teaching require the hard work of seeking to understand the realities of children's lives and to respond in ways that extend from those contextualized understandings. Movements with children across class-specific identities and practices are frequently uncertain and imperfect. These movements, too, are histories, with complicated trajectories.

I would wish for Laurie and other girls like her some of the things that are seen as part of critical literacy pedagogies. I would hope that alternative classroom spaces could open up even more room for Laurie to explore boundaries between the values of home, community, and school. The power and resilience of working-class women in the face of often-crushing economic hardship are things I think Laurie had begun to value, even as she expressed her resistance toward the women at home who embodied those strengths. Her own kindergarten brassiness may have been an early manifestation of working-class values that may serve Laurie well. Someday, she may face the economic struggles lived by her mother and the ensuing subjectivities that reflect how women live the material and political realities of working-class life in the United States. A more overt focus on the politics of media, literary texts, and social events would be a stepping stone toward helping Laurie and other girls prepare for the challenges they will face in an increasingly dichotomized economy. Girls such as Laurie need to find safe classroom spaces for living but also for challenging the femininities that are shaped through attachments and practices in their homes and neighborhoods. The starting point for critical classroom practice is girls' own words and experiences— words that echo the values of their mothers and other loved ones. Working-class girls can take up new practices of literacy as they form relations with middle-class teachers and take the risks involved in trying out new practices and identities. This is a kind of multiplicity that reflects the situated locations of students and teachers. Teachers have to contend with their own class specific histories and the feelings they evoke, as the girls they teach learn which kinds of fictions will be safe to write, voice, and live in school.

✺ 5 ✺

Boyhood Stories and Practices

"Bobby [Labonte] and I are maybe a little different than some of the other brothers in racing," said Terry [Labonte]. . . . "I mean, we actually like each other and get along good. It was pretty special today, it really was."

"Yeah," said Bobby, "taking a victory lap together was about the coolest thing we ever did."

"Second coolest," said Terry.

"What?"

"The time we shot Dad's pickup was the coolest."

"Oh man, I'd forgotten about that."

Like little boys giggling over some adolescent romp, they told of the day when their father's battered old pickup simply gave up, and of their decision to do the humane thing and put it out of its misery by filling it full of bullets. How times have changed. Little more than half a century earlier, this would have been the two devilish whiskey-running cousins from Dawsonville, Lloyd Seay and Roy Hall, having run one-two in a Sunday race at dusty old Lakewood Speedway in Atlanta, now sitting around a stove at the Pure Oil station and recounting tales of outsmarting the sheriffs hiding in ambush along the old highway leading from the stills of Dawson County to Atlanta. But maybe times hadn't changed at all. For at the heart of the matter, then as well as now, it was all about dashing young men and their racing machines.

—Paul Hemphill, *Wheels*

JAKE WAS THE SECOND of the two children whom I came to know over the 3-year period of my research project. If ever a research collaboration were to have the potential to effect educational change, this study of Jake seemed like the time and the place. Jake's family was extremely interested in my research observations of him. His family contributed significantly to my understandings of Jake's responses to school. As the study evolved and Jake began to experience difficulties in school, his mother used information from the project to conference with his teachers. At the close of Jake's kindergarten year, Mrs. Thompson, Hope Longwell-Grice, and I had spent two days examining the materials we had collected about Jake. The result of our teacher–researcher analyses were hundreds of pages of transcribed dialogue, which we condensed into a summary we thought would be useful for Jake's family and his future teachers (see Appendix). Jake's mother used this summary in her discussions with teachers at the primary school he attended.

That this collaborative project had, in the end, minimal effect on Jake's educational experiences speaks to the dissonances between institutional practices of schooling and working-class values. The practices and values Jake experienced at home, where he was a successful learner, were—beyond kindergarten—significantly different from classroom learning practices. Performing segmented tasks, often while seated; engaging in activities that involved two-dimensional paper-and-pencil work; providing commentary or explanations about an activity that was already *done*—these were practices that were valued in school. Social practices at home emphasized just the opposite: moving freely from one activity setting to another; learning by doing, not by talking about parts of a task; engaging in constructive activities in which printed text was connected to three-dimensional objects. During his kindergarten year, Jake was able to move freely around the classroom, engaging in practices that were closer to those he experienced at home. In first and second grade, however, he encountered practices that were much farther removed from his experiences and values. My history of Jake's engagements with literacy moves between these two cultural locations. Home visits with Jake and his family, the teacher–researcher dialogue constructed after his kindergarten year, and classroom observations of Jake in grades K–2—all are threaded into stories of Jake's boyhood.

Unlike the close relationship I formed with Laurie because of the time I spent with her in a tutoring role, my observations of Jake were more like those of an educator with a certain degree of outsider status. Jake knew that I was not his teacher. He insisted at one point to members of his family, when being teased that he was so bad in school he had to have a teacher follow him home as well: "She ain't my teacher!" He and his family accepted me in a role that was somewhere in-between a school professional and a naive academic, willing to be educated herself as she also tried to help Jake have the best possible educational experiences. My relationship with Jake was also influenced by differences of gender. An image that recalls that difference is one of watching him play Sega video games. During many of my home visits, I watched as Jake became ab-sorbed in action video games: football, car racing, the Lion King. I can recall feeling a sense of relief when Jake put on a Sega game that involved manipulating a dolphin figure, befriended by a benevolent blue whale. I read and composed Jake's life as a woman (see Miller, 1986), working hard to understand passions and interests that in many cases I did not myself share. In that sense, our relationship was typical of instances in which a female teacher engages with the particulars of a young boy's life, aiming to understand them from the situated location of her own experiences. My narrative begins with readings of Jake's kindergarten year, where "action" was to become a leading metaphor within his history as I came to know it.

KINDERGARTEN APPRENTICESHIPS

An image from Jake's kindergarten year: Jake is working at the Puzzles Center, putting fireman clothes and paraphernalia on Fireman Dan. While he is working, Jake begins to tell a fantasy story involving Fireman Dan, and he includes me in the story. I ask him if he wants to draw a picture of the story. He shakes his head as if saying, "Of course not." About 2 months later, I am again observing Jake at the Puzzles Center. This time he is putting together a puzzle, something he has often chosen during Centers. Some of the other children working at this Centers table have been drawing pictures. I ask Jake if he would like to draw something. He responds, "There's nothing to draw for me."

In many respects, kindergarten was a resounding success for Jake. Because of the open-ended nature of many kindergarten practices, Jake was able to construct connections with school on his own terms. He engaged with classroom practices in kindergarten in ways that mirrored his modes of learning at home. Jake moved freely and independently among Centers—"roaming," as Mrs. Thompson described things in our review of his kindergarten year. He often chose to work with three-dimensional tasks, preferring practices that involved building things and putting together puzzles. However, for much of his kindergarten year, Jake resisted activities that involved two-dimensional texts, such as read-ing or pretend-reading; writing, drawing, and dictating stories; or using numbers. As with his response to my efforts to nudge him toward drawing a story, his early responses to symbolic activities involving drawing, writing, or reading were often ones of blunt noninterest. During whole-class read-alouds, for instance, Jake often sat in the back of the rug area, not participating verbally in the choral reading activity. Jake could become passionately engaged in activities that were of interest to *him*. Our instructional efforts to engage him in more school-like literacy practices, however, were often met with the firm "no way" kind of response that I encountered at the Puzzles Center. As Mrs. Thompson commented about Jake in kindergarten, "He's always on task; it just might not be your task."

Jake's responses to academic tasks in his earliest weeks and months in school were reflections of boyhood values and social practices lived at home. In the context of his family life, Jake was a gifted learner. He rapidly appropriated the knowledge and skills valued by family members, especially those valued by his father—a talented and successful mechanical contractor and carpenter. Jake brought his strengths as a learner to his kindergarten classroom, where he experienced the greatest success of his primary school career. His engagements with classroom expectations sometimes created conflict for him even in kindergarten. Jake's preference for constructive action rather than verbal narration, writing, or drawing created moments in which he bumped up against institutional expectations. On the whole, however, his kindergarten year seemed a happy moment in Jake's life in school—a time and space where on his own terms he began to engage with classroom literacies. Toward the end of the year, standing in line in the school cafeteria in a practice run of buying and eating lunch in first grade, Jake turned with a huge smile on his face and announced, "Guess what, I can read!" Along the way to that bit of self-awareness, Jake spent his kindergarten year moving between worlds of family intimacy and apprenticeship learning at home, and the newness of classroom practices. The apprenticeships he experienced at home as a young boy were things he could also enact in the social spaces of kindergarten.

Those family relations, values, and social practices are an appropriate beginning point for the story of Jake's coming to know and be in primary school. Images and reflections from home visits with Jake set the stage for later discussions of his engagements with school discourses. The details of his life at home provide a context for understanding how his connections with school discourses entailed conflict as well as hopefulness. The forms of action and knowledge that Jake embraced were strongly tied to gendered identities in his family and community. Growing up as a young boy in a blue-collar setting, Jake expressed his identification with the values of the men in his life and the literacies that men practiced in their work and family relationships.

Love and Independence

Some images from home visits with Jake and his family evoke the loving relationships and yet expectations for independence that shaped Jake's early learning experiences. On a chilly winter day during his kindergarten year, Jake had gone out back to show me how he could hit plastic softballs, sometimes all the way into neighbors' yards. Lee Ann, his younger sister, was playing on the wooden swingset that happened to be in range of Jake's flying softballs. I voiced concern about her getting hit, but Jake's father, standing nearby, assured me, "Don't worry, she's really tough." On a later visit in the fall of first grade, Jake was learning how to play umpire in a batting session with his father and some neighborhood children. He insisted on standing close behind a girl batting, in part because he wanted to bat himself. Warning Jake in a no-nonsense tone that he had to stand back, Jake's father said gruffly, "He's gonna find out himself." Jake and Lee Ann were not treated as young "students," in need of explicit education and constant protection. As Jake's mother voiced her family's philosophy of teaching and learning: Children need to learn from their mistakes, to learn for themselves. Minor bumps and mishaps along the way were an accepted part of how Jake and Lee Ann learned through participation in family life.

Extended family members—grandparents, uncles, aunts, cousins—were a part of Jake's home on a day-to-day basis. Neighborhood children were also frequent visitors to Jake's home. Social spaces in this home were therefore typically buzzing with talk and activity. One of Jake's two grandmothers or a visiting cousin might be sitting in the family living room, watching TV or chatting with his mother, as Jake and his sister (and later a baby brother) moved freely from one activity to the next. Amid these fluid relationships, the task of caring for Jake was shared among family members during his early years in school. Jake's maternal grandmother, or mom-mom, was an especially important person in his life. Jake spent the night at his grandparents' home during kindergarten. That way, he could sleep a little later in the morning since he attended the afternoon kindergarten program. As Jake's mother put things, what he didn't get from her in terms of caretaking and love he got from his mom-mom.

The ways in which Jake and Lee Ann participated as members of their family reflected differences in age, since Lee Ann was about 3 years younger than Jake, and gender. Both children were treated as independents who could figure out things for themselves, given a reasonable degree of support. Each received open expressions of affection from family members. However, their identities as family members reflected the ways in which gender was lived in their home. Lee Ann's bedroom was painted in pastel colors and outfitted with a toy stove, replica kitchenware and china, and baby dolls. For Halloween during Jake's second-grade school-year, Lee Ann dressed up as a fairy. That same Halloween, Jake had dressed up as a NASCAR driver, wearing the yellow and red Kellogg's racing colors worn by his personal favorite, Terry Labonte. Jake sometimes played with Lee Ann's kitchen toys, just as he occasionally chose the house symbolic play area during Centers time in kindergarten. More typically, however, he embraced traditional roles connected with men and older boys. The birth of a baby brother in the summer after first grade created an important new relationship for Jake. He bonded intensely with the new baby, Brad, carrying him around the house and entertaining him with gestures and funny faces.

Growing up within this close-knit family, Jake seemed most drawn to the identities lived by his father, a sometimes gruff, or "direct" (as Jake's mother teasingly noted), man. Jake's father was a self-taught man—a ninth-grade dropout who had subsequently learned through reading and apprenticeships the professions of carpentry and mechanical contracting. He was a gifted carpenter whose backyard shed was the workspace of an artisan. Its walls were intricately lined with tools and wood materials, and a large powersaw was placed in the middle. Jake also had a powersaw, and he sometimes worked alongside his father, cutting small pieces of wood or painting objects his father had made. Jake demonstrated the use of his powersaw during my first tour of this carpentry workshed. I watched (at first horror struck) as he stuck his finger in the vibrating needle that cut wood but not small fingers. Jake's workspace in the shed was set up so that he could work alongside his father. However, in no sense was this required of him. Jake chose this activity as one of many things he shared with his father. Jake also joined his father in a family passion for car racing and the collection of miniature replicas of racing cars. In his parents' room was his father's huge collection of race car miniatures, each displayed with a picture of the car's driver. Hung in Jake's bedroom was his own smaller collection of race car minia-tures. As early as his kindergarten year, Jake could identify each NASCAR vehicle and its driver by "reading" such details as racing colors and insignia, the shape of different cars, and print.

A scene from a first-grade home visit: Jake's mother and his mom-mom are sitting with me in the family living room, having a chat about Jake and his responses to school. Jake's grandmother tells the story of how Jake's dad educated himself, after dropping out of high school, through reading manuals and then practicing his crafts. He could have gone into any number of professions, she noted; he was gifted in a number of arenas. Jake, too, was a gifted learner, she added as our conversation went on. She commented that Jake would be his own person, after I asked what she thought Jake would do later in life. Jake would probably end up doing not one thing, but different things. She noted how quickly Jake picked up knowledge and expertise at home—things like helping put together the family swimming pool. These words voiced about Jake echoed themes from his father's life story: independence, giftedness as a learner, reluctance to box himself into a single profession. These stories of father and son were prominent themes in Jake's life in kindergarten and integral aspects of the values he was later to bring to first- and second-grade practices of reading.

Learning Through Action

At home, Jake "roamed" among activities that suited his evolving interests and goals. Like his father, Jake was almost constantly in motion, sitting down only to perform a specific task, then moving on to the next activity. Jake was more than capable of sustaining interest in a project. His energy and movement did not prevent him from engaging in more reflective activities such as reading (Jake often listened to books read by his mom-mom), painting wooden objects made by his father, or figuring out how something worked (Jake sometimes joined his father for house repairs and even some mechanical contracting jobs). However, sitting down for long stretches of time to talk or read ran counter to his preferences. In Jake's family, women were more likely to engage in sustained talk in the living room or at the kitchen table while his father finished tasks around the house. In a conversation we had in Jake's second-grade year in school, Jake's father commented that he, too, could not sit still for long. Jake got this trait from him, he suggested. Sustaining interest in an activity also required that the task make sense. A task had to be something that needed to get done. Otherwise, as Jake would sometimes later voice about school activities, it was just plain "stupid."

In his kindergarten classroom, Jake similarly roamed among learning Centers, doing activities that engaged his evolving interests. The open-ended organization of the kindergarten curriculum allowed him to be in control of his own activity. Even in whole-class activities on the rug, Jake was able to sit in the back of the group and participate as he felt comfortable or engaged. During Centers, he generally focused on constructive activities that involved working with objects—wooden blocks, puzzles, Lego blocks, plastic building materials. As Mrs. Thompson observed in our child review of Jake, he seemed to view school learning as a series of performed actions. His social entry into a Center was not verbally announced, nor was his ongoing work explained or "frozen" by verbal commentary. The one exception seemed to be a love of storytelling; Jake sometimes set off spinning a fantasy narrative as he worked with manipulatives (such as puzzles) or played outside on the playground. Even his narrated fantasies, however, were rooted in physical action. Jake's narratives are an important window onto the discourses that helped shape his response to literacy practices in school. Those primary discourses (Gee, 1996), so closely tied to the practices Jake lived at home, can be seen in the Max stories he created on the school playground, in his engagement with Sega games at home, and in his performance of a NASCAR story in kindergarten.

Boyhood Fictions

During his kindergarten year, Jake had not one but two fictional dogs: Max 1 and Max 2. He was perfectly able to distinguish Max 1 and Max 2 when asked which Max was present at a particular time. Out on the playground, Jake would throw one of his dogs a ball, follow the trajectory of the ball with his eyes, and then run at full speed if Max tried to run away with the ball himself. It turns out, as Jake's mother explained one day, that Max 1 was a fictional representation of the real Max, a beagle who belonged to Jake's teenage cousin. The real Max would sometimes come along when Jake's cousin visited, and the children present would pursue as Max outran them easily. Max 2 was a dog of Jake's fictional creation. In second grade, Jake composed in his Writer's Notebook a story that reflected his desires for a Max of his own.

> *WRITER'S NOTEBOOK ENTRY (11/26)*
>
> TOday i myt get a Dog. a Begt
> i am name hem max
> becuase my
> cosint haves a Dog so i want a
> Dog i am going to the Farmrs
> makit to get my Dog today
> and wan i came
> home i will thaek
> ham for a wak
>
> (Today I might get a dog, a beagle. I am naming him Max, because my cousin has a dog so I want a dog. I am going to the Farmer's Market to get my dog today. And when I come home I will take him for a walk.)

As a boy growing up, Jake's fictional worlds seemed largely construed around texts involving a high degree of movement, and often media forms. A special passion of his were Sega video games. He had acquired a Sega player for Christmas in kindergarten, and action games like the

Lion King, car racing, Sonic the Hedge Hog, and football games were media games that Jake loved. During my home visits, he demonstrated his command over various Sega games, his whole body becoming engaged in the physical action as he manipulated the Sega controls and tried to avert the disasters that loomed for characters such as Sonic the Hedge Hog. Descriptions from one such set of observations in the fall of Jake's first-grade year evoke these media practices:

> As soon as we entered Jake's room, he insisted on showing me a sample of his current collection of Sega video games. The first video game he inserted into the Sega player was a football game. Jake was able to choose which teams to set against one another, and he clicked on the 49ers versus the Dolphins. I was not able to follow all the rapid movements of his choices on the controls; he used the controls to decide tackles and other movements. During the Sega football game, Jake was extremely physically active. His verbalizations ("I tagged him," "I pushed him down") were uttered in the voice of one actually engaged in the game itself. Jake seemed to be on the field *with* the football players, his whole body moving with each hit. After Jake had played through a few football tackles, he switched to a race car video. In this video game, the action occurred from the point of view of someone inside a car. The video game was constructed as if the player were inside the car, looking out at the rapidly passing landscape. At various key points in the "race," there would be an obstacle to avoid in order not to crash. Rather than what I would picture as a race track, the course was set in a landscape area—with hills, trees, etc. Jake was once again physically engaged in his enactment or performance of the video game. He used body movements and loud sound effects to perform the movement of the race car. He was the driver of the car, maneuvering it through the dangers of the race course. At one point, a slightly older visiting cousin, Cheryl, commented that Jake was always loud. A very physically engaged and vocal player was certainly on view during these Sega games. (Fieldnotes)

Gilbert and Gilbert (1998) argue that such electronic and video game cultures are typically linked to discourses of masculinity. Video games like the ones played by Jake are marketed for young boys to play, and boys find the games exciting and fun. Boys get to experience "playing the body" (Gilbert & Gilbert, p. 78) as a means of practicing the male identities that they will perform outside of video game contexts. Gilbert and Gilbert read such practices through a critical lens, pointing out how such video games can position boys in hegemonic discourses of masculinity. These discourses align masculinity with "power and aggression, with victory and winning, [and] with superiority and strength" (p. 72). As Gilbert and Gilbert argue:

> Although some girls do play and enjoy electronic games, electronic gaming is constructed predominately as a male activity and a male field of pleasure. Just as the "Barbie" culture constructs a highly gendered representational field targeted at girls, the "Game Boy" world of video games offers much the same to boys and young men. Through participation in the multimedia practices associated with electronic gaming, boys and young men enter into a discursive field in which constructions of hegemonic masculinity dominate, and within which they can practice and play at masculinity, and at what it comes to represent. (p. 73)

Video games did become a way in which Jake performed the masculinities typical of media-influenced social words. Important to an understanding of the passion that Jake felt for Sega games, however, is the connection between the action games and home practices of living. The Sega games reflected values that Jake lived in a class setting in which action was for men an important part of knowing.

Toward the end of Jake's kindergarten year, I decided to interview Jake and his classmates in pairs or small focus groups. From a methodological perspective, this attempt to interview kindergarten-age children was largely a failure. A few children expressed their response to our request that they reflect on their kindergarten learning experiences by breaking out into song and dance. Others sat stiffly, responding as though they were on a television talk show. We decided to continue with these interviews even though we could see their methodological flaws, since occasionally children did respond in ways that added something new to our understandings of them. Jake's response to this interview was one such moment, becoming a lens into the discourses integral to his presentation of self in story form (Scollon & Scollon, 1981). His fictional representation of boyhood identities drew richly from media culture. When contrasted with the expectations of school literacy practices, his performance also reflected important differences between home and school language practices. Jake's enactment of a NASCAR story speaks to possible tensions between the identities he valued as a kindergarten student and the language practices connected to talking, being, and knowing in school. This analysis of Jake's narrative is the final thread in my history of his kindergarten learning experiences.

That history turns momentarily to an analysis of another narrative performance, this one from a very young speaker: the 2-year-old daughter of anthropologists living in an Athabaskan community in Alaska. The analysis by Ronald and Suzanne Scollon (1981) of their daughter Rachel's storytelling was set within a larger study of cultural discourses and modes of self-presentation among the Athabaskans. Rachel's narrative presentation of self was used to point out the ways in which, even as a 2-year-old, she had begun to appropriate modes of narration grounded in middle-class literacy practices. When constructing a narrative about herself and her baby brother, for instance, Rachel recast those involved as characters, using narrative framing devices, third-person pronominal forms, and past-tense forms. She also cast herself in an *authorial* position, one more distanced from the here-and-now of real events. An excerpt from a narrative recounted by Rachel illustrates this mode of storytelling. An analytical focus on intonation and breath contours rather than grammatical phrases is represented in the Scollons' (1981) transcription of Rachel's spoken text:*

> Once upon a time there was a girl named Rachel and
> there was a boy / named Tommy //
> the went f-
> for a walk and there was Da-/
> .) ddy
> he went for a walk too //
> They
> -ey wrote a-
> letter
> down to
> Baby Tommy's
> Grandma //
> she
> Baby Tommy had a n-
> Baby Tommy had a
> fish xxx //
> she
> and he had a Mom //
> and his Mom

---

*The following conventions are used in the transcription of Rachel's narrative (see Scollon & Scollon, 1981, pp. 66, 71). A new line indicates a pause. A dot indicates a breath and a pause. A right parenthesis followed by a word indicates that the word was said with an ingressive airstream. A hyphen indicates an interrupted word. A single slash indicates a nonfinal falling intonation. A double slash indicates a final intonation that is a high rising then falling contour.

told him
to read his story //
and his Mom
m-
tell him No! //
You
got to sleep
and then
Baby Tommy went to sleep (pp. 74–75)

Scollon and Scollon quote Hall (1973) in arguing that we are all authors of a continual autobiography. Rachel's emerging autobiographical text fictionalizes the self and others in ways characteristic of what Scollon and Scollon refer to as *essayist literacy*—the text forms and genres that draw on literacy as opposed to orality. As they contend in their discussion of Rachel's narrative performance:

> We would argue then that Rachel had understood by this time the essential distance of authorship from text. The character in regard to the author is a different person. It is a decontextualized person. It is a person who exists in relationship to the text and the events told in it. This person bears a third person relationship to the author and this consistent maintenance of the point of view is one of the hallmarks of written text. (p. 70)

In other words, part of what constitutes literacy practices, even for a 2-year-old long before she has begun to "read," is the construction of an *authorial self*—a narrator who shapes characters and events from a perspective one step removed from present or past experience. Literacy practices, then, entail the appropriation of certain kinds of textual forms and also the appropriation of certain ways of negotiating discursive boundaries between self and other, past and present (see Dyson, 1993). Two-year-old Rachel, argue the Scollons, was already strongly immersed in cultural practices drawing on middle-class essayist literacies, and she had begun to "author" her own autobiography accordingly.

I return now to Jake's performance of a NASCAR narrative and the autobiographical work he accomplished. Recall that Jake's performance was set in the context of an interview in late spring of his kindergarten year. Jake and a classmate whom he had chosen to accompany him, Marty, were seated in a classroom not in use at the time. I videotaped their responses to a series of interview questions about their kindergarten year, which was nearly over, and their expectations about first grade. Prior to Jake's narrative, both boys had talked about moments from their kindergarten year when they had suffered a physical mishap. Minor scrapes

and bruises on arms or knees were woven into stories of past experience,
such as the story of being pushed by an aggressive classmate. Sensing an
opportunity to see how the boys would construct a fictional text, I shifted
the task to one of making up a story. Almost immediately, Jake got up
and began enacting a race car story in which he voiced an authorial role
that put him in the middle of the action. He was both the driver of a car
and the narrator of events. My transcription of Jake's story* includes
details from his physical movement, these being central to arguments
about how he drew on discourses that differ in important ways from
Rachel's narrative presentation of self.

DEBORAH: I want you to tell me a # a make believe story that you
make up
of all [*Jake gets out of his chair*] the things {that you can make
up # you -

JAKE: {I can make up
{race car smackin' into the wall
DEBORAH: {can you um
Jake can you tell it here # [*pointing to his chair*] because {the
camera's
JAKE: {or
would
DEBORAH: can you sit here [*leans forward and touches Jake's chair*]
and tell it
Jake comes back into view of the video camera
{tell your story
JAKE: {or you can [*Jake moves backward to sitting position while looking at the point off camera he was just depicting*]
or you can smack one race car into the wall [*he points to the
wall with his left hand*]
and you can just leave 'im there and just go around the turn
*Jake indicates how the race car travels by pointing with his left hand
and moving it in a wide arc to the right*
DEBORAH: is that your story?

---

*The following conventions are used in the transcription of Jake's narrative. A space symbol
(#) indicates a pause. A comma indicates a very short pause or breath intake. A curly bracket
indicates overlapping speech. Italicized words indicate emphasis. Italicized sentences or
italicized phrases in square brackets indicate movement as opposed to speech. A hyphen
indicates cut-off speech.

JAKE: I'll show you how the track looks like
      Jake gets up from his chair, still looking at Deborah, and points in the direction of the fictional track
      you start from here
      Jake begins making a wide circle around the classroom
      you go a*round* # and a*round* # and a*round* # and a*round* [*circling the room*] and a*round* # and a*round*
      and this track can up, down, and smack into the wall
      Jake walks back toward his chair
DEBORAH: okay
JAKE: [*laughing*] I did that on my race car before [*sitting on the edge of his chair*]
MARTY: {guess what
JAKE: [*standing up quickly*] {like [*makes high-pitched engine roar, moving forward with his torso tilted forward and stiffened*]
      my car caught on fire [*Jake comes back toward chair*]
      and I jumped out
DEBORAH: okay
MARTY: guess what [*Jake sits down*]
DEBORAH: {let me
JAKE: {guess who ca- # guess whose car I crawled on?
      Terry's [*Jake sits upright in chair, with a wide smile on his face*]
DEBORAH: Terry's car # {caught on fire?
MARTY: {le(t')s le(t')s line up
JAKE: no # {no
MARTY: {line up Jake
JAKE: maybe I jumped on [*Jake looks upward toward ceiling*]
MARTY: Jake Jake [*touching Jake's chin*]
JAKE: maybe I jumped on
MARTY: Jake [*touching Jake's chin*]
JAKE: maybe I jumped on Earnhardt's car [*Jake smiles*]
DEBORAH: hmmm

I entered into this moment of social negotiation expecting to hear Jake tell a "story"; that is, a school-like enactment that represents the self and others as fictionalized characters and that voices a certain authorial distance. Clearly, his agenda was different from mine. Our competing agendas are reflected in my failed attempts to get Jake to "tell his story" from where he had been sitting, so that his story would be captured on the video camera. Instead, Jake insisted on a physically enacted performance.

Asked to tell a "make-believe story," he created an imaginary race track, using gesture and movement to narrate the fictional scene. At one point in this enactment, Jake circled around the classroom to show how the track was configured. In his description of the track, Jake remained close inside the action, taking the listener with him as he demonstrated the track's spatial configuration. His actions and verbalizations recalled for me his Max narratives out on the playground or his engagement with Sega games. These narrative performances shared a proximity of *self* as narrator to *self* as character within the action. When contrasted with Rachel's narrative enactment, Jake's performance shaped a different set of relations between the fictional worlds of the story and the experiential worlds voiced by the narrator. Jake's imaginative shaping of a NASCAR scene was something that he practiced in ways evocative of his use of Sega controls, his "roaming" among activities at home, and his creation of Max 1 and 2 fictions.

About midway through this performance, Jake shifted into narrating some events at the track. This was marked by his utterance, "I did that on my race car before." Momentarily, he sat down as he uttered this phrase, perhaps in tacit acknowledgment of my efforts to nudge him toward a more school-like textual performance. Almost immediately, however, he stood up and began engaging in an experiential narrative. His body became tilted forward and stiffened as he became a race car, roaring as it moved ahead on the track. Then he positioned himself as a driver on the track, narrating (using first-person forms) that "my car caught on fire and I jumped out." The remainder of Jake's story tells how he (the race car driver) jumped onto Terry (Labonte's) car, and even maybe onto Earnhardt's car. This heroic escape from death may have been narrated slightly tongue-in-cheek. Dale Earnhardt was the favorite driver of Jake's mother, who participated in NASCAR activities even though, by her account, she was not crazy about doing so.* In portraying himself as jumping out of his own burning car onto Earnhardt's still-moving car, Jake may have been parodying a driver whom he liked to refer to as "stupid." Such sparring about different drivers was a family ritual, and Jake made it no secret that his driver was Terry Labonte. Thus, the heroic move of jumping onto Earnhardt's car was part of the ongoing autobiographical work being accomplished in this performance.

---

*Dale Earnhardt, known in NASCAR circles as "The Intimidator," is believed by some to have been the greatest stock car driver ever. Earnhardt was killed after the completion of the research study described in this chapter, when his Number 3 Chevy crashed at the Daytona International Speedway on February 18, 2001.

Though richly imaginative, Jake's performance drew on a set of rhetorical strategies that were different from Rachel's. Jake's performed narrative drew on *action* as a way of telling. Set within school-like discourse practices, Jake's enactment resisted those practices that I, voicing a teacher's identity, asked him to perform.

Schooling in the primary grades should ideally become a set of opportunities for children to experience new identities connected with textual practices. Dyson (1989, 1993) describes how children from diverse communities can engage in practices that both draw on and also extend or "pluralize" the means by which they mediate the boundaries of self and other, written text and embodied action. Rather than giving up the cherished identities they live at home, students like Jake should be able to place those identities in dialogue with new ones. The instructional movement toward such cultural and class pluralism, however, requires first that the learner's primary values, language practices, and identities be valued in the classroom. Without the acceptance within the classroom walls of students' primary discourses, ethnically diverse and poor and working-class students are faced with the challenge of appropriating language practices and values that may seem unfamiliar or unwanted. For Jake to engage with the kinds of literacy practices valued by school, he would have to see a space for the things he most valued. Instruction that allowed for movement between practices would for Jake require that his self-reliance, preference for three-dimensional symbolic activities, and valuing of embodied action be valued aspects of school. Responsive schooling for Jake would entail an acknowledgment of his identity as a member of a blue-collar family with its particular expressions of masculinity.

As my history turns to Jake's engagement with first- and second-grade literacies, it will be clear that just the opposite occurred as the curriculum became more formal and demanding. In kindergarten, there was space for Jake to interact with school literacy practices on his own terms. In first and second grade, Jake's self-reliance and reluctance to engage with school literacy practices began to be seen as forms of resistance. The young boy who was so gifted a learner at home increasingly distanced himself from classroom values and social practices. Jake's story beyond kindergarten is one of increasing resistance and struggle, even as he made significant strides in coming to know and be amid classroom discourses.

COMING TO KNOW AND BE IN TWO DISCOURSE COMMUNITIES

Being the quick study that he was, Jake figured out early on in first grade how to "do school." In late September of first grade, I observed Jake as he was awarded the Star of the Week award for good behavior. Different children presented Jake with pictures and comments about him. Marty, who had been placed in the same classroom as Jake, proclaimed that he and Jake were friends. Another boy drew a picture of race cars; still another child drew a picture of Jake fishing. At the close of Jake's Star of the Week session, Jake's first-grade teacher, Mrs. Rhodes, articulated the behaviors that would lead to getting the award: somebody who follows the ABC rules, does a good job, and always does his or her work nicely.

Two contrasting images stand out from observations of Jake in the early months of his first-grade year. One is drawn from classroom observations in mid-October, during the language arts activities often done in the morning hours. Children had been asked to create a "story wheel" (using pictures representing the story's plot) based on the story "Franklin in the Dark" from their literature anthology. As I rotated around the room, I observed Jake flipping through a Toys 'R Us catalogue, then putting his head down on his desk to indicate he was finished. Some of the children had written the title of the story on the front of their story wheels. Jake wrote the title and also inserted apostrophes into every word in the title. He was drawing on an earlier whole-class lesson on the use of contractions, and possibly also replicating the use of contractions he saw in the title of the Toys 'R Us catalogue. Mrs. Rhodes came over to see Jake's work, looking in amusement at how he had appropriated contractions in his own writing. Well aware of the adults' response to his writing, Jake let out a muted "lion roar," something he had done frequently in kindergarten as an expression of power and bemused resistance.

A second image is drawn from a home visit with Jake and his family. On a sunny day in early October, Jake, Lee Ann, and some neighborhood children were in front of the house playing softball. Jake's father was momentarily pitching, with different children taking turns at batting. What Jake's mother referred to as the "other Jake" became visible to me. He was physically expressive of anger in ways never seen in the classroom. When Jake missed a pitch from his father, he tossed the baseball bat across the yard toward his dad. When he didn't want to assume the role of umpire with a neighborhood girl at bat, he contorted his body in an expression of outrage. Later, during the batting, Jake "attacked" his father in anger, tackling him by grabbing onto his legs. At times like these, Jake would often let out a roar, not unlike the "lion roar" he occasionally voiced in the classroom, but louder and more expressive. These physical expressions of outrage seemed theatrical and half-teasing. Standing next to me as we watched Jake's antics, his mother commented that *this* was the Jake she saw at home. She noted that Jake had a hard time controlling his temper and often expressed his anger physically. We both recalled how Jake had recently won the Star of the Week award and how well behaved he acted in school. His mother added that Jake had told her that he didn't want to get "tickets" for bad behavior.

Early in first grade, Jake figured out the system of behaviors that would keep him from getting tickets and also gain him favor with his teacher. He learned how to follow the ABC rules, an important part of the school's ideology that was closely followed in his classroom. Children recited the ABC mantra of behaviors each morning, along with reciting the Pledge of Allegiance and having a moment of silence. Jake participated in these practices and adopted them as means of gaining kudos from his teacher and avoiding unpleasant things, such as missing recess. Much like Laurie, he wanted to be "good" for his first-grade teacher. In these ways, Jake was adept at learning how to participate in two discourse communities. Within the intimacy of family relationships at home, he expressed a rambunctious identity. He could be loud and quite physical. In the classroom, Jake assumed a more subdued persona. His softened version of the "lion roar" and his willingness to do what was needed to get a Star of the Week award indicate his success in learning how to "do school" in first grade.

Jake's success with these institutional values, however, did not guarantee a connection with school literacy practices. Reading difficulty surfaced in first grade, even though Jake was a participant in frequent interactions with books at home. His mom-mom read to him and Lee Ann nightly during his kindergarten year, when he spent nights at her house. His grandmother was an avid reader who loved to share her own collection of books with Jake and Lee Ann as well as read the school's "reading train" take-home books to them. His home was full of books—children's books purchased through a mail-order service and informational books tied to adults' particular areas of interest. The reading of literary texts and children's books was largely practiced by women in Jake's family. His mother and grandmother read Danielle Steele and similar novels as well as children's literature. Informational and especially historical texts were more the province of Jake's father, reflecting his interests in the JFK assassination and his own family history. These reading practices at home are important lenses for understanding Jake's history as a reader and writer in school.

Reading Practices at Home and School

A literary image comes from my observations of Jake at home in first grade: On a sunny fall day, I am introduced to the first Charlotte, a large spider sitting in its web spun along the side of the swimming pool. Jake's mother asks him to recite the spider's name, and then asks for the names of other characters in the children's book *Charlotte's Web*. Later on that same afternoon, I meet the second Charlotte, who was to narrowly escape demise from a softball hit by Jake. This second Charlotte has spun a web under the eaves of the front porch.

Literary references threaded into ongoing experience and talk about a love of reading were an important part of Jake's home life during his primary school years. His childhood was richly informed by the literary interests of his mother and grandmother, and by his father's passion for historical and informational books. In his bedroom was a bookshelf full of children's books, such as Dr. Seuss books and beginning children's readers that his mother ordered from a mail-order service. Some of these mail-order books came with "sight word" flashcards using words from the text. Frequently, adult family members noted how much Jake loved to read himself. His identity as a reader seemed to be embedded in a family valuing of reading for enjoyment and information. Jake was also viewed as a quick study with computer literacies. His family had acquired a computer for their mechanical contracting business. During a home visit early in Jake's second-grade year, Jake at his father's prompting demonstrated his facility with the computer. He worked with an educational CD-ROM program that featured the *Sesame Street* character Elmo. He read menu options that were displayed with pictures and text. During that same home visit, Jake's mother told me that Jake had gone to bed the night before to read some car-racing magazines. He had fallen asleep almost immediately, she noted, exhausted from the new routines of the school year.

When I made a late fall visit to Jake's home during his second-grade schoolyear, Jake's father told me how he had become a local expert on JFK assassination theories. He said that he read voraciously, mostly books about the JFK assassination. He went on to recount an incident in a bookstore in which a store clerk had referred a customer to *him* for information about JFK books. He told this story with a twinkle in his eye, teasingly noting how he, a working man, was considered an expert in this literary domain. He added that he owned a ton of books on the JFK assassination. Jake appropriated these male practices of reading as the starting ground from which he approached classroom reading. In his second-grade Reader's Workshop, for instance, Jake hovered for days around *Happy Birthday, Martin Luther King*, a book about the history of King's civil rights activism and his eventual assassination.

Images related to these literacy practices emerge from having observed Jake reading at home. On an earlier home visit, in April of his first-grade year, I am sitting in the living room and talking with Jake's mother and his grandmother about reading. I suggest that Jake needs to do a lot of reading over the summer, to help him get ready for second grade. Jake's mother tells me how much Jake loves to read. His mom-mom adds that Jake holds back in school and notes his giftedness as a learner. Jake's mother pulls out an informational book about U.S. presidents and begins quizzing Jake about presidents and other political figures. She asks such questions as, "Who was the second president?" and "What did George Washington chop down?" At one point, Jake seems to be reading from an appendix that lists presidents and facts about them. He seems to make use of some print cues to read or pretend-read presidential facts. Other facts seem to be ones he knows from memory. When his mother asks him a question about the Black man who was shot, Jake responds from memory that it was Martin Luther King. All the while, Jake holds the informational book in his lap, occasionally consulting it to support his responses.

Jake's reading at home, however, did not always connect easily with classroom reading expectations. Comments in March of first grade stand in contrast to Jake's ebullient comment in kindergarten, "Guess what, I can read!" During the early-morning activity time, when children completed morning papers and read books from the classroom collection, I noticed Jake looking at a copy of a Berenstein Bears book, *Prize Pumpkin*. Berenstein Bears children's books typically have text–picture relationships that are difficult for emergent readers. I asked Jake if he could read the book, and he shook his head "no." Later during the morning paper period, I noticed Jake sitting with no book at all. I approached him and asked whether he could find a book that he could read from the classroom collection of books. He responded, "I don't know how to read any of them." During DEAR time, I noted the titles of books that Jake "read": *Tyrone* and *Berenstein Bears and the Green-Eyed Monster*. I asked Jake again whether he could read his book as he was looking at the Berenstein Bears book. He said, "I can't read none, I can't read none."

Jake's frustrated comments in early spring of first grade were an honest reflection of his difficulties with reading in school. While he was viewed as a gifted reader and learner at home, by mid-year in first grade Jake was struggling academically in school. However, his self-reflections in early March were contradicted by his fluent reading of books such as *Pumpkin, Pumpkin*—books with more supportive text–picture relationships. Outside of such supportive practices, Jake readily stumbled or tuned out amid classroom literacy practices. Part of the problem seemed similar to one that Laurie also experienced as an emergent reader in first grade. Many of the mid-year selections in the school's first-grade

anthology series were beyond Jake's reading abilities. Jake was just beginning to make strides as an emergent reader in kindergarten, reading
predictable books like *Rain, Rain* confidently. He needed more time to
solidify his strengths and fluency with similar books in first grade before
moving on to more difficult texts.

Equally as difficult for Jake, however, were the ways in which school
reading practices differed from those in his family life. Reading practices
in school included whole-class readings of anthology selections, independent reading during DEAR, and a variety of skills activities designed to
go along with the children's anthology selections. For Jake, many of
these activities must have seemed senseless. Adult members of his family
occasionally asked him to display his reading prowess or computer proficiency, particularly when a visitor associated with school was around the
house. However, reading at home was more typically immersed in the
ebb and flow of work, play, and family relations. Jake listened to stories
when spending nights with his grandmother in kindergarten and first
grade. Literary connections were made in relation to spiders who had
spun webs around Jake's home. Race car magazines and informational
books were typical of the books that Jake read in ways that mirrored his
father's interests. When Jake encountered classroom reading practices
that emphasized analyzing parts of texts—graphophonics, and word or
genre structures—he sometimes seemed disengaged or frustrated. In response to a morning paper activity in December requiring him to find
and circle "hidden words," for instance, Jake found one word and then
floundered with the rest. In May of that year, when asked to fill in a
"story map" worksheet with plot information from the story "Strange
Bumps" (a selection in Jake's anthology series, reprinted from Arnold
Lobel's *Owl at Home*), Jake seemed perplexed. "I'm not sure what it is,"
he commented in frustration. "What *what* is?" I asked, trying to figure
out how he was responding to the story map activity. "This *paper*," he
said.

In second grade, Jake encountered reading practices that harkened
back to his kindergarten year. The Reader's Workshop in Mrs. Williams's
classroom seemed well suited to Jake's independence and modes of reading. Although Reader's Workshop had bounded requirements, there was
a considerable degree of latitude. Children could move about during
Reader's Workshop, stretching out on the rug, sitting in a rocking chair,
or huddling in a corner by themselves. As long as he was reading, Jake
could choose books of interest to him, at his individualized comfort level
in terms of text difficulty.

Within the Reader's Workshop, Jake did make significant strides. He
started off the year in second grade reading predictable texts such as

Spider Spider from the Sunshine series for emergent readers. By January, however, he was reading beginning chapter books such as *Frog and Toad* and informational books such as *Hockey Is Our Game* and *Happy Birthday, Martin Luther King*. During Reader's Workshop, Jake often sequestered himself in a corner, defining himself as an independent in ways evocative of his kindergarten year. He alternated between choosing narrative texts, such as *Popcorn*, *Caps for Sale*, and *Frog and Toad*, and informational books. Samples of his book choices in the latter half of the schoolyear reflect these typical reading preferences:

January 16	*Happy Birthday, Martin Luther King*
February 6	*Hungry Hungry Sharks*
March 13	*Hockey Is Our Game*
April 24	*Mr. Putter and Tabby Pour the Tea*

Although Jake ended the schoolyear having made enormous gains in school reading practices, he was still about 6 months behind peers who were on target vis-à-vis grade-level expectations. Toward the end of the schoolyear, when more successful readers in his classroom were reading short novels, Jake was still working with short informational books and beginning chapter books. His accomplishments as a reader in second grade, though impressive, did not match up with an expected sequence of achievements. Jake was to enter third grade as a fragile reader amid the expectations and practices that constituted reading in an institutional sense. And yet the layered complexities of Jake's history as a reader do not begin or end with reading competencies, as important as these might be within an institutional setting.

In September, I observed as Jake participated in a thematic unit on communities, including the buildings that made up different communities. Mrs. Williams was reading aloud *Up Goes the Skyscraper*, a book that chronicles the construction of a skyscraper. Mrs. Williams's discussion with children about the text drew on phrases and concepts from construction and engineering. I noticed that Jake, typically distant and disengaged during such book discussions, was alert and engaged. Some of the text and pictures depicted the construction of heating and air conditioning systems in the new building. At one point, Jake raised his hand and commented that his father worked as a heating and air conditioning repairman.

Jake struggled to align school reading practices with his life as a reader at home, including the gendered relations that shaped reading amid the intimacy of family life. His history at home certainly did not preclude becoming a reader in school. However, the cultural practices that defined classroom reading made it more difficult for Jake to read successfully in school. Like other things in his family life, reading had to make good sense to be something of value to Jake. Adult men in his family and community did not bother with practices that were not linked to constructive action or informative learning in the context of social, political, and historical events. Jake searched to find a place for himself amid school literacy activities, and he was only partly successful in doing so. At home, he continued to be a brilliant young apprentice learner. In the classroom, he increasingly began resisting the values that defined being a successful student. Resistance and tuning out became a safer route than giving up his passions and identities, and perhaps the comfort of more familiar kinds of knowledge. Apprenticeship learning at home, increasing resistance at school—these were strands of Jake's biography as he moved closer toward being a third grader.

Family Apprenticeships and School Literacy Practices

During a home visit in April of Jake's second-grade year in school, I toured the bedroom that he and Lee Ann shared. As we entered the room, I was struck by NASCAR images. The previous year the walls had been painted a bold blue color, and a black and white checkered wallpaper border (at chair rail level) had been added. This was quite a striking effect, one that Jake's mother warned could get to you if you stared at it for too long. The hanging shelf with tiny compartments for Jake's collection of NASCAR miniatures was still there. NASCAR sheets were on the top bed of a bunk bed set, where Jake slept. NASCAR posters showing images of drivers and cars lined the walls. While we were in his bedroom, Jake pulled out a Super Speedway Strategies game from under the bed and demonstrated how it worked. It was not surprising, then, when Jake composed in his Writer's Notebook, "When I grow up I like to be a nascar driv."

A classroom conflict in November involving NASCAR miniatures became a moment when Jake's difficulties with school practices became visible. By late fall of second grade, Jake had routinely begun to tune out or fantasize when classroom practices were difficult or unfamiliar. On this particular morning, the children had returned to the classroom after time in the library and were chorally reading a selection from a poetry anthology. This was a collection of poems suitable for second-graders compiled by Mrs. Williams. During the whole-class poetry reading, Jake began playing with a NASCAR miniature inside his desk. Earlier, he had propped up the NASCAR miniature on his desk while composing in his Writer's Notebook. Wanting him to fully experience the poetry reading and ensuing literary discussion, Jake's teacher walked by and confiscated the tiny car. Later that afternoon, when I walked over to help Jake edit a piece of writing, he blew up. "I *hate* school; I *hate* teachers because they boss you around," he announced, his entire body expressing his rage. From Mrs. Williams's point of view, at times like these Jake was becoming difficult to deal with in the classroom. She viewed his tuning out and resistance as stubbornness about doing his work. He seemed easily distracted, wanting only to play. From Jake's point of view, it was becoming increasingly difficult to maintain an interest in school literacy practices. As reading and writing drew on more extended texts that included literary language and poetic imagery, he struggled to find points of connection. Reflections I wrote shortly after this moment in the classroom note the increasing conflict that Jake was experiencing as he moved between the worlds of home and school, negotiating his place within them.

> In the context of having visited Jake at home and having seen the enormous value of these [NASCAR] miniatures for him and his father, I can see the tiny race car as a symbol of what he most values in the world. I think that, for him, the car is a connection point, something he can put before him on the desk and use as a prop of sorts as he is engaging in the difficult job (for him at least) of writing. I suppose the problem (for Mrs. Williams, other teachers, even Jake) is that the car does not necessarily lead him toward writing. He does not want to symbolically *represent* the car and racing; he wants to *live it experientially*.
>
> I suppose I see more and more disengagement, bordering on resistance, as I observe Jake in his second-grade classroom. During whole-class discussions, he tends to sit back on the rug area, as was his pattern as early as kindergarten. However, he seems more emotionally disengaged (or am I only noticing this more?). Yesterday in class, Jake looked a bit scruffy and uninterested in general. I saw him become more engaged when reading in Workshop (he read the book *Small Pig* quite fluently, which really surprised me; it seems like just 2 weeks ago he was reading books such as *In a Dark Dark Wood*). Overall, however, I'm seeing Jake position himself outside the culture of formal schooling, both physically (sitting far away from Mrs. Williams) and emotionally (resisting writing unless he can connect it immediately to the worlds he most values). He seems to love people in the classroom. I'm sure he cares about Mrs. Williams and other teaching adults. Only 2 weeks ago he gave me an "I love you" note. But he clearly does not like a lot of what he has to do. . . . I cannot help but think back to conversa-

tions with Jake's father, who seems to represent the life worlds
that Jake so deeply cares about. (Fieldnotes)

Two additional memories come from classroom observations in second grade. In early December, Jake puts his head down on his desk and
pretends to fall asleep during a math activity in which children are doing
"take away" problems. As I walk by him to note what he is doing (and
to try to figure out why), he whispers a story to me: The night before,
his father awoke him in the middle of the night to take him along for a
heating repair emergency. Jake's words are, "I had to" [i.e., I had to be
up all night]. He is aware that he is losing it with respect to maintaining
a focus on the math activity, and his fantasy reflects a reasonable explanation, consonant with family values, for why things would be so difficult
right now. Another image comes from an observation in March. Jake had
been having a lot of trouble in school that week. For days, he had written
nothing in his Writer's Notebook. Mrs. Williams had expressed her concerns that week that he was reading on a late-first-grade level in second
grade. After a class read-aloud of a chapter from the children's novel *How
to Eat Worms*, I try to gain a better understanding of the meaning that
Jake is making of late-second-grade reading practices. During the read-
aloud, he had put his head on his desk, seemingly disengaged—though
I wasn't sure. After the read-aloud, as children are getting ready for lunch,
I ask Jake if he was listening and what he was thinking about when he
put his head down on his desk. He *was* listening, Jake assures me. He
tells me how he was thinking of the time when he went fishing and threw
out a line with live bait. He demonstrates physically, enacting the motion
of throwing out the fishing line.

Things were not dramatically different for Jake in terms of the connections between the identities he lived within his family and those valued
in school. What was different was that the stakes were getting higher.
In kindergarten, there was more room for Jake to express his bemused
resistance and independence. He could walk away from a Center and
simply choose one more to his liking. Rarely did he tune out during
kindergarten activities; he could be constantly in physical motion, much
like at home. By second grade, social spaces and practices were more
bounded and constrained. Within those bounded practices, Jake's options
were more limited. He continued to express open and trusting warmth
toward adults. He typically had a huge smile on his face upon entering
the classroom each morning. Alongside that trust in adults, however, was
an increasing dislike of academic practices—and on occasion the teachers
who insisted upon them. In second grade, Jake began telling family members that he didn't like school, and he began resisting doing his homework.

I asked Jake during a home visit in April what the story was with his homework. His response evoked earlier comments about tasks that seemed useless: "It's stupid." I watched as Jake wrestled with a homework assignment that required him to make up sentences to go with weekly spelling words (e.g., *sitting, learning, thinking*). Jake dictated some sentences to his mother, a compromise suggested by Mrs. Williams to make Jake's homework less of a nightly chore. Even so, it was clear to me that Jake was doing his homework in a half-mocking and distant way.

At the same time that Jake was struggling with academic practices in school, he was thriving as a young apprentice in family hobbies and in his father's business. In kindergarten and first grade, Jake had helped with home projects such as putting together a large Christmas train set and building a backyard swimming pool. In second grade, he had begun to accompany his dad on repair jobs when it seemed appropriate to bring him along. By this time, his family had started their mechanical contracting business, and Jake had been named vice president (his mother was the office manager and secretary; all in the family were part owners and business partners). Sitting at the kitchen table after the more tedious chore of getting through homework, Jake's mother shared thoughts about the future. Jake needed to learn to read well to go on to college, she noted—following my comment that he needed to read over the summer to get ready for third grade. Jake replied quickly and firmly that he would not go to college. Passing through the kitchen, Jake's father added his 2 cents worth: Jake would take over the family business. As if in enactment of this story voiced about him, Jake picked up the phone nearby and began demonstrating how he answered calls for the family business.

The stories voiced about us, by those whom we most love and value, shape our identities in ways more powerful than even the most authoritative institutional systems of social regulation. Caught between discourses at home and school, deeply committed to the relations and values lived within his family, Jake struggled to negotiate a space for himself as a young reader and writer in the classroom. He practiced school literacies— sometimes giving himself up to the task of writing about car racing or family events, sometimes reading books reflective of his interests. Storylines voiced about him in his family, however, often seemed a stronger pull, a more powerful shaping of his boyhood identities. Faced with substantial risks when confronted with challenging school practices, ones that would require him to think and be in new and unfamiliar ways, Jake chose what must have seemed a safer route: Tune out, fantasize, resist; then go home to live the relations that were so warmly embracing. That there was sometimes room in second grade for Jake to enact the identities he valued at home is testimony to the skill and compassion of his teacher.

In his Writer's Notebook and in other classroom locations, Jake did seem to find a way to move between class identities. Though Jake could not physically perform his fantasies in the spaces of his Writer's Notebook, he could live them imaginatively and shape them into written form. His written compositions suggest the hopefulness of living between discourses. They also recall the regrettable fact that literacy education so rarely addresses the relations of gender and class that shape children's literate engagements.

WRITING BOYHOOD IDENTITIES

In May of second grade, Jake and his classmates participated in a lengthy science unit on insects and metamorphosis. Children studied the life cycle of a butterfly, observing and documenting how a tiny larva grew into a caterpillar, created a chrysalis, and emerged as a butterfly and flew away. During the unit, children recorded their observations in science diaries. I made the assumption, based on what was by that time nearly 3 years of research, that Jake would love to talk and write science. I thought that the focus in science education on action and exploration would be a much closer fit to Jake's experiences as a learner at home. I had told his family members and Mrs. Williams that I hoped science could be a point of connection for Jake. This was a hopeful interpretive reading of Jake's possibilities for engaging with school literacies, perhaps one that also drew on stereotypical images of working-class boys finding an "in" to school through science. Images come to mind, for instance, from the British documentary film 35 and Up, which chronicles the lives of a number of children at 7-year intervals, beginning in primary school. In it, the viewer meets one young working-class boy who grows up in the country, exploring the natural world around him. Later, the boy finds his identity in school through science, becoming a science professor in adulthood. Was this a possible story for Jake, a boy who was so passionate about construction activities and mechanical relationships?

What disrupted this imagined narrative was Jake's response to the talk and writing that constituted science in his second-grade classroom. As scholars of classroom discourse such as Jay Lemke (1990) and Judith Green and Carol Dixon (1993) argue, *science discourse* is not a single set of activities and discourses, but multiple discourses and roles enacted within particular classroom communities. The ways in which science discourses are enacted in classrooms vary, dependent on the activities and undergirding philosophies that are practiced. In Jake's second-grade classroom, science was strongly connected with Mrs. Williams's valuing of extended reading and writing. To her credit as an accomplished teacher of literacy, she brought science into dialogue with language arts. Children learned about science through talking and writing in ways facilitated by Mrs. Williams and consonant with the school district's mandate that certain kits be used to teach science. These science kits came with supplies, teachers' instructions, and journaling worksheets that encouraged certain kinds of science talk and writing. Mrs. Williams focused children's science diary writing during the insects and metamorphosis unit by providing a purpose for writing, often that of describing changes in the larvae/caterpillars kept in small plastic containers.

For Jake, writing science became another location for resistance. He seemed to enjoy observing the life-cycle changes of the caterpillar he kept on his desk during the unit. The bounded nature of science diary writing, however, was something he found useless—in his words, "dumb." His responses to an interview (conducted by a science education colleague, Nancy Brickhouse) about his science diary reflect the ways in which writing in school could be constraining and tedious. Still, Jake's comments about Writer's Workshop express multiple interpretations of what school literacy practices mean to him. Reading and writing are valued practices as long as he can participate in them in relatively unconstrained ways, such as the ways in which writing is construed in Workshop:

> NANCY: So how do you feel about it [science diary writing]? Do you enjoy it?
>
> JAKE: See, I don't like it. I have to go [mumbles word] . . . because you know when I'm in the middle of a story she always calls out, "Go and get your reading things" or "Go get your spelling insects journals" or I don't know what they call it . . .
>
> JAKE: [*Talks about a similar frustration he sometimes has when trying to finish a book in Reader's Workshop*]
>
> NANCY: So what does that have to do with your insects journal?
>
> JAKE: She always interrupts me if I'm in the middle of something.
>
> NANCY: So how do you feel about this kind of writing rather than what you do in Writer's Workshop?
>
> JAKE: See, Writing Workshop's lots of fun. Guess what, this is dumb.
>
> NANCY: So why do you like Writer's Workshop?
>
> JAKE: Because you can write stories about anybody you know, and like, where you went and why you get to go.
>
> NANCY: So it's because you can write about anything you want to?
>
> JAKE: Yeah.
>
> NANCY: So why is this dumb?

JAKE: Because like if you're in the middle of a story or something
she ain't going to help you and she calls you and passes out
dumb things.

I think the word *dumb* has multiple meanings for Jake: constraining,
difficult, useless. What comes to mind are his performances of stories
(e.g., Max 1 and 2, Sega, NASCAR) in kindergarten and how these differ
from the confines of science diary writing in second grade. The practices
that constituted *writing* in Workshop afforded a bit more space for the
kinds of textual enactments he valued. Jake could at least engage with
the passions that shaped his life at home. In that sense, Writer's Workshop
was what Anne Haas Dyson (1993) refers to as a *permeable curriculum*—
more open to hybridity. Writing in Workshop came closer to helping Jake
negotiate home and school identities. Jake's compositions reflected his
efforts to negotiate locations between the richness of family life and the
more unfamiliar demands of school.

Jake's Writer's Notebook compositions in second grade begin and
end with scenes from family life. Real experiences and fantasies based
on those experiences are a predominant theme in his Notebook. Though
defining himself as an independent within the social spaces of home and
school, a self-reliant young apprentice, he wrote stories in second grade
reflecting an identity strongly tied to others. A recurrent theme in his
stories is the bond he formed with his baby brother, Brad. The two brothers
are portrayed in Jake's stories as sharing a world of boyhood—playing
softball, celebrating birthdays, and just hanging out together after school.

WRITER'S NOTEBOOK ENTRY (12/4)

me and my brother
Brad we play
togather at home
it is fun thet I
have a brather
like thet I
Lave hem aned
Day I came home
and wana I'm dana
my homework
i play whan hom.

(Me and my brother Brad, we play together at home. It is fun that
I have a brother like that. I love him and [every] day I come home
and when I'm done my homework I play with him.)

WRITER'S NOTEBOOK ENTRY (2/24)

in June it is
me and my brother
Brads brthbay
my brothrs brthDay
is the 21 min
is the 19.
i will trne 8
my brothr will trne
1 in June

(In June it is me and my brother Brad's birthday. My brother's
birthday is the 21st. Mine is the 19th. I will turn 8. My brother will
turn 1 in June.)

WRITER'S NOTEBOOK ENTRY (5/15)

Me and Brad play baesball
out fraint in the grss
and Brad hits home runs
and i hit home runs to
I hit the ball ovar
a van the ball allmost
hit the van. Brad hit
the samft ball it hit the wndoe
of the van. but it didn't
bast the wndooe on the van
at my house in the drivway.
the red mieni van wndooe
it hit the van tier
the wandooe I feal cool and
i faet like the big boys.

(Me and Brad play baseball out front in the grass, and Brad hits
home runs and I hit home runs too. I hit the ball over a van. The
ball almost hit the van. Brad hit the softball. It hit the window of
the van. But it didn't bust the window on the van at my house in
the driveway, the red mini-van window. It hit the tire [not?] the
window. I feel cool and I felt like the big boys.)

Sharing experiences of boyhood, being a big brother in relation to
Brad—these storied images convey Jake's sense of self. Being cool like
one of the "big boys" means being able to hit the ball over the family

van. However, even this demonstration of power and control is tied to an experience jointly shared with his young brother, a novice baseball hitter. Views of selfhood and knowledge are written into this narrative of family life, Jake's younger brother learning in ways reminiscent of Jake's own apprenticeships. Minor mishaps are part of the package of learning through action. The van parked in the driveway can tolerate a few softball hits along the way.

Not surprisingly, NASCAR experiences are a recurring theme in Jake's Writer's Notebook. NASCAR fictions were for Jake important means of shaping his cultural experience within the rhetorical forms valued in Writer's Workshop. The activities and passions shared by father and son play an important role in Jake's NASCAR stories. In entries composed on two consecutive days in December, Jake wrote about past and anticipated NASCAR-related events. Scenes evocative of the excitement of car racing and collecting mingle with the requirement of composing a written narrative.

WRITER'S NOTEBOOK ENTRY (12/9)

yesdrday i want
to [store name]
it is a racing stor
me and my bab we go
to the stor to go
to get nascar sthav
and pay for it thend
we go home to pat
it in oro rooms
wana war don
we eat Banra then
we go to bud

(Yesterday I went to [store name]. It is a racing store. Me and my dad, we go to the store to go to get NASCAR [stuff?] and pay for it. Then we go home to put it in our rooms. When we're done we eat dinner then we go to bed.)

WRITER'S NOTEBOOK ENTRY (12/10)

to day me and my Dad
ar going to Airport Speedway
to see me pract
af i Do good I

will get money
[unintelligible text]
then we go
home

(Today me and my Dad are going to Airport Speedway to see me
practice. If I do good I will get money. . . . Then we go home.)

Often, Jake's Writer's Notebook narratives place him in the midst of
a family experience: a trip, a family holiday, an outing on a boat. Jake
recounts past experiences within his family life, sometimes reflecting on
his feelings when encountering the unfamiliarity and challenge of new
social possibilities. His depiction of a trip he took with his father to visit
some relatives in another state, for instance, recounts both the excitement
of this adventure and his longings for the warmth of being home with
his mother and younger sister.

WRITER'S NOTEBOOK ENTRY (1/7-1/9)

last summr
i want to North
Carolina it [was?] June
1rs. it was a laga ride
i was tighred and
hagrye and the
nast Day we warae
in [missing word?] i wans happy we
had a [unintelligible word] we
get hatdogs then we
want to Bad i was
sleeping like a mase
I hrda strana nosis
wana i want i
mast my mom and
my littl sastr i
was sad to leav
my house avre
night and side
to my mom i like to
came home bekasse
i wanta to came home

(Last summer, I went to North Carolina. It [was?] June 1st. It was a long ride. I was tired and hungry. And the next day we were in [missing word]. I was happy we had a [unclear word]. We got hot dogs then we went to bed. I was sleeping like a mouse. I heard strange noises. When I went [i.e., away] I missed my mom and my little sister. I was sad to leave my house every night and said to my mom, I like to come home because I want to come home.)

In some recountings of family trips, Jake takes on an adventurous and heroic fictional role. In a story that draws from his experiences of going fishing with his grandparents in the summer, Jake portrays himself piloting a boat. Recalling his kindergarten enactments of driving a race car, Jake's boating narrative fictionalizes him as boldly jumping into the driver's seat and happening upon a boat race. In his story, Jake wins the race and triumphantly makes his way back to shore.

WRITER'S NOTEBOOK ENTRY (1/14)

last summr i want
to the beach it
whars fun. we go
boat rideing in the
sea i briv the boat
i hop in the set
and brov away from the
bak i want fast
i run into a boat
roce i win the race
and brive the boat
boak to the bak.

(Last summer I went to the beach. It was fun. We go boat riding in the sea. I drive the boat. I hopped in the seat and drove away from the bank. I went fast. I run into a boat race. I win the race and drive the boat back to the bank.)

Similarly, Jake composes in a story written earlier in the school year (in early December): "last summr i want to virginia with my mom mom i saht a trky." (Last summer I went to Virginia with my mom-mom. I shot a turkey.)

That these writing practices in school helped Jake gain greater access to the particular literacies valued in primary school is unquestionable. Two contrasting Writer's Notebook entries illustrate the distance Jake had traveled by March in terms of his understanding of the rhetorical practices, genres, and conventions that constituted writing in second grade. In a late September and early October set of entries, Jake composed a set of formulaic "I like . . . because . . . " texts about dogs and school.

WRITER'S NOTEBOOK ENTRIES (9/30 AND 10/1)

I like dogs because they are good to people and people like dog because you can play with them.

I like school because they do work because it is fun and kids go to school.

By March, Jake's entry about astronauts in space reveals a much more sophisticated understanding of classroom writing practices. For this entry, Jake worked for a week on a narrative about the Apollo space missions. He drew on the textual styles of informational books in the classroom; one of Jake's favorite books around this time was a book on astronauts and their space missions. He had undoubtedly read about the Apollo 13 astronauts' close encounter with disaster in their attempt to land on the moon. Appropriating the rhetorical style of information books (although confusing some factual details), Jake recounts stories from the Apollo missions.

WRITER'S NOTEBOOK ENTRY (3/6–3/14)

First Men on the Moon
    [The] first men on the moon were Buzz Aldrin and Neil Armstrong and Jack Swigert. And then I had a feeling that they would not make it to the moon. But they made it to the moon. It was Apollo 12. The people had to hurry to get back to earth before the men ran out of oxygen and power but the men were to get to the shuttle and they found out the men had enough time to get back to earth. They were halfway back to earth and then the men made it back to earth just in time.

Such contrasts as these speak to how Jake connected his life worlds at home with writing practices in school. These school practices were things he had come to value; in his words, writing in Workshop was "lots of fun." Fictions composed in his Writer's Notebook seemed situated somewhere in between home and school identities. Jake could write about his experiences and interests while appropriating rhetorical forms that aligned him with literacy practices valued in second grade. I have wondered at times, however, how such writing practices could have been extended to include new forms of boyhood heroism. Although the pages of his Writer's Notebook were hopeful pedagogical spaces, possible sites of critical inquiry, they remained isolated moments of connection with school textual practices. Jake needed to know and feel new forms of *action* in school, as he maintained the blue-collar identities that he so strongly valued. My concluding comments reflect on the possibilities for such cultural change to occur within the pedagogical spaces of primary-grade classrooms.

NEGOTIATING CLASS IDENTITIES IN SCHOOL

Literacy education for working-class children is sometimes viewed as a process of helping children move *from* more familiar language practices of home and community *to* the more unfamiliar textual practices of the classroom. Children from working-class communities, it is argued, can experience painful cultural conflict in their primary-grade classrooms. Through a process of apprenticeship learning or more direct instruction, and sometimes both, children from working-class communities have to gain access to the discourses of middle-class institutions. Various theories and methods have been brought to bear on the problem of how to help poor and working-class children, including those from ethnic-minority communities, better gain access to institutional literacy practices. Genre instruction advocates, for instance, have argued for the explicit teaching of textual forms, in a direct challenge to the premises and methods of whole-language pedagogies (see Cope & Kalantzis, 1993; Reid, 1987). Other literacy educators have argued for explicit teaching of skills and strategies, in an effort to afford culturally diverse learners access to the discourses of institutional power and control (e.g., Delpit, 1995). Literacy educators working toward social justice and equity have argued that something must be done to equalize children's opportunities in classrooms and the workforce. Jake and students like him must gain access to school literacies if they are to succeed in school and in the workforce. Everything from political slogans (e.g., Success for all children) to school curricula are predicated on this metaphor of learning as appropriation, even mastery. This is a hopeful democratic ideal.

Jake's history contradicts the premises of this utopian metaphor. The chances that he would have readily taken up school discourse practices as things of unquestioned value are just about nil. More realistic was the history that did evolve: Jake held on to the identities and forms of practice arising out of his attachments with members of his family. As academic practices became more demanding, home and school became increasingly disparate life worlds. Compared with the richness of apprenticeship learning at home, school just couldn't compete. Jake's comments about home-work (*it's stupid*), science diary writing (*dumb*), and school in general leave little doubt as to where his allegiances lie. Still, his story as a young reader and writer reveals spaces, openings, where critical change was possible. Jake's Writer's Notebook suggests gaps in a too-easy narration of his ability and willingness to embrace school literacy practices. The difference between these writing practices and those of science diary writing was the possibility of hybridity. In his Notebook, Jake could give voice to the boyhood experi-ences and fantasies that he valued while still participating in a school literacy practice. Jake bought into school reading practices when he could bring them into dialogue with his most powerful boyhood attachments.

My reflections on Jake's history in grades K–2 could be taken as an endorsement of a specific curriculum. Some might infer this from the story of how Jake seemed happier in his second-grade Reading and Writing Workshops than in the more traditional literacy curriculum in his first-grade classroom. Parts of this reading would be an honest reflection of what seemed to work for Jake. Because he valued self-reliance and free-dom of choice, the pedagogies embraced by his second-grade teacher seemed better suited to his needs. In Reader's Workshop he was able to read informational texts as well as begin to explore chapter books reflec-tive of his changing reading abilities. In Writer's Workshop, he was able to write about NASCAR events, family relationships, and boyhood adven-tures. His mother, a woman who strongly voiced her views about educa-tion to me and Jake's teachers, expressed her preferences for this kind of curriculum. At the beginning of third grade, when things began to get very rocky for Jake in school, she expressed dismay that he couldn't continue to read at his own pace. What did it matter, she asked, that Jake was reading differently from some of his classmates? Her philosophy of teaching reverberated throughout the history of this research project. As a literacy educator trying to increase Jake's chances for success, I urged that same kind of philosophy. I shared notes and observations. Jake's teachers and I brainstormed how to help him buy into school values that would shape his opportunities down the road.

Although I can echo the concerns of Jake's mother and voice my allegiance to her philosophy of education, Jake's history as told in this chapter suggests even deeper areas of concern. At the close of his kinder-garten year, Mrs. Thompson, Hope Longwell-Grice, and I tried to figure out what to recommend to his future teachers. We could even at that early point see the writing on the wall. With the increasing constraints of first- and second-grade work, including the requirement of more seat-work, Jake would suffocate. Among our recommendations was one that Jake participate in literacy activities that bridged home and school cultures. His kindergarten teacher suggested a scrapbook as an intermediate kind of literacy practice. Recall that even at the close of Jake's kindergarten year, he was still not choosing to work at the Writing Center and he was just beginning to enjoy books for emerging readers, such as *Rain, Rain.* Mrs. Thompson's insightful suggestion evoked an issue that I now see as fundamental to improving Jake's chances for success in school. To bring about the critical change that we, as teachers, demanded of him, educational practices would have to be at least partly situated in the life worlds that Jake so strongly valued. The whole-language adage of "write about the topic of your choice" opened up a fissure between blue-collar practices of living and learning and middle-class education. Still, Jake needed more sustained opportunities for negotiating such boundaries in the classroom.

Jake's family had this figured out long before I did. His dad told me that schools *could* be engaging environments for learning. All they had to do was find ways to connect students' interests with academic tasks. Math could be taught with NASCAR miniatures just as easily as blocks. What was frustrating for me as a literacy educator trying to advocate for his son was the thorny question of how to help make this happen in a real-life, complex situation. Jake's first- and second-grade teachers cared about him and were committed, experienced educators. Still, I wasn't sure how to work in collaboration with them to respond to Jake's increasing distress and disengagement in school. I no longer view the answer as one of finding yet a better instructional method. I believe that Jake would have balked at explicit genre instruction, for instance, as strongly as he resisted his spelling homework. His problems lay more in conflicts between an institutional *system* of middle-class practices and the life worlds he embraced as a boy. For his opportunities to change in school, a deeper process of change would be required. The risks of that kind of change are many, as it involves political struggle. To make space for Jake's primary values in school would mean opening up the curriculum to the forms of knowledge voiced by working men like his father. The classist nature of schools and society at large pretty much guarantees that won't happen.

The language philosopher Mikhail Bakhtin (1981) argues that there are always spaces for critique, within even the most authoritative discourses. Working-class students and families, and even middle-class classroom teachers, are located within hegemonic discourses that can be demeaning and disempowering. The possibilities for activism can seem limited given societies' tendencies to silence those who are already living on the margins of middle-class power structures. Students such as Jake are incredibly resilient, savvy at negotiating meaningful locations for themselves in the spaces that do emerge in otherwise disengaging school practices. As critical ethnographer Kathleen Stewart (1996) argues, a space "on the side of the road" is an important metaphor for thinking about such moments of connection. A Writer's Notebook opens up space for living a NASCAR fantasy or expressing one's love of family. Given his resourcefulness, I have every bit of confidence that Jake will lead a happy, productive life. The knowledge that is valued in his family will, I am certain, support him even through rocky years of school. As a critical literacy educator, however, I am compelled to work for more than an isolated case of resilience and strong family support. Laurie's even more troubling experiences in primary school have made me acutely aware of how much schools need to change if students such as Laurie and Jake are to experience the sense of belonging in school that they experience with loved ones at home. How devastating it must be for the reverse to occur—for children to feel themselves to be outsiders in their own classrooms.

The gaps for critique and response that Bakhtin describes are evidenced in the teaching practices of courageous educators. Behind closed doors (or open ones, if they have a sympathetic building administrator), teachers find creative means of helping students negotiate boundaries of race, class, ethnicity, and gender. They risk opening up classroom spaces to children's primary values, passions, and identities. At an institutional level, schools like the Richmond Road School in Auckland, New Zealand (see Cazden, 1992), provide compelling evidence that schools can embrace community values and thrive as hybrid cultural spaces. The kind of linguistic and cultural hybridity for which Kris Gutiérrez and her colleagues argue (e.g., Gutiérrez et al., 1999; Gutiérrez, Baquedano-López, & Tejeda, 2000; see also Anzaldua, 1987) was in this remarkable school connected with structural organizations and material practices rooted in community life. Having in recent years become involved in such activist schooling, in a working-class neighborhood far from where Jake and his family reside, I hold out hope for the possibility of such permeable teaching communities. The best resources for creating them are not particular methods of instruction or curricular materials, but extended dialogues and educational collaborations with community members. Families and grassroots community leaders can help show us the way. They can help us extend our understanding of critical literacy education to include *them* in the teaching practices we construct with students and in the research practices we create with our literacy education colleagues.

ಜ 6 ಜಿ

Hybrid Languages of Inquiry

Real social relations are deeply embedded within the practice of writing itself, as well as in the relations within which writing is read. To write in different ways is to live in different ways. It is also to be read in different ways, in different relations, and often by different people. This area of possibility, and thence of choice, is specific, not abstract, and commitment in its only important sense is specific in just these terms. It is specific within a writer's actual and possible social relations as one kind of producer. It is specific also in the most concrete forms of these same actual and possible relations, in actual and possible notations, conventions, forms and language. Thus to recognize alignment is to learn, if we choose, the hard and total specificities of commitment. (Williams, 1977, p. 205)

—Raymond Williams, *Marxism and Literature*

THE TEXTS COMPOSED BY literacy researchers are rhetorical acts of meaning construction, as socially situated as any other material practice. To imagine that things are otherwise would be to distance the educational research profession from some valuable dialogues about the texts that shape our social practices and communities. The historian Natalie Zemon Davis (1987) uses the term *fictions* to refer to the literary shaping of events through storytelling and other rhetorical practices. Using this term as a wider metaphor, the texts that help constitute the educational research community are fictions—shapings that reflect our histories and aspirations. Moreover, the texts we write as educators embody considerations of value; as Joanne Pagano (1991) argues, they are *moral fictions*. They express and reveal what is important to study, and they place (often implicitly) value on certain ways of theorizing about the problems or questions we study. Throughout this book, I have constructed a dialogue between literary readings of working-class childhoods and educational research on literacy practices. My reflections in this final chapter consider the implications of creating educational research discourses that are literary in form, or that draw on hybrid genres of writing. What are the implications of such rhetorical choices? What sorts of alignments with theory, research, or social activism do they express?

My reflections occur amid a long history of narrative studies in the social sciences, where an interest in rhetoric and storytelling has accompanied a shift toward viewing academic practices as interpretive and textual (e.g., Clifford & Marcus, 1986; Davis, 1987; Edel, 1959/1984; Geertz, 1974; Ortner, 1984; Rosaldo, 1989; Taylor, 1985a, 1985b). In the field of education, narrative inquiries have become important to theory and research ranging from studies of psychology to studies of curriculum. There is a vibrant and growing literature on narrative as a "mode of thought" and a means of constructing knowledge (Bruner, 1986, 1991, 1996); a lens for theorizing about teachers' knowledge and contextual practices (e.g., Clandinin & Connelly, 1996; Middleton, 1993); a means of engaging teachers and student teachers in critical reflections on curriculum (e.g., Grumet, 1988; Miller, 1996; Pagano, 1991) and through which students construe gendered identities (Davies, 1993) and moral selves (Tappan & Mikel Brown, 1989); and, more generally, both method and metaphor for educational inquiry (e.g., Barone, 1992; Carter, 1993; Casey, 1995–96; Witherall & Noddings, 1991). My emphasis in this landscape of narrative inquiry turns to the commitments entailed by rhetorical choices. As my story unfolds, it becomes once again a mingling of literary and essayist forms, moving between narrative histories and reflective commentary on the situated nature of writing, teaching, and theorizing.

I take as a point of departure the argument of philosopher Martha Nussbaum (1990), who writes that there is a relationship between the rhetorical form of philosophical inquiries and the problems, questions, and theories such inquiries produce. Nussbaum uses early Greek drama and philosophical writing (1986) and contemporary literature (1990) as vantage points from which to consider connections between literary form and philosophy. Her discussions of the values and conceptions of knowledge suggested by literary texts are important ones for educators to consider. Rarely do educational researchers challenge the social relations shaped within their rhetorical practices. Nussbaum's arguments about literary texts as modes of philosophical inquiry can focus attention on these kinds of questions.

Nussbaum's arguments center on aspects of experience that typically remain oblique in social science discourses. I want to focus on what she terms *love's knowledge*—knowledge between persons and of persons. The textures of literary discourses, she suggests, are especially revealing of a kind of relational knowing that is part of everyday life. I find problematic Nussbaum's tendencies to relegate knowledge of and between subjects to a *kind* of knowledge. Later in this chapter, I turn to Bakhtin's writings as a framework for thinking about how all knowledge occurs as a social relation between subjects. Still, Nussbaum's writings provide a useful beginning point, since they are focused on the implications of literary form for processes of inquiry. I discuss some distinctions she makes about a view of knowledge suggested by the multilayered textures of literary discourses. I consider the possibility of viewing this as a metaphor for situated understandings. I then turn to an exemplar of educational research writing that draws on literary genres, asking whether Nussbaum's description of knowledge seems an appropriate way of capturing some important commitments expressed in Mike Rose's (1989) book *Lives on the Boundary*.

Narrative discourses, suggests Nussbaum, focus readers' attention on how relations between subjects engender changes in identities, beliefs, practices, and understandings. New relationships can constitute new forms of knowledge—some empowering, some tragic. Much of what subjects come to know is enmeshed in the particulars of those relations. Understandings of other individuals (as in the cases of friendship and love) are therefore exemplary of the ways in which social relationships can be constitutive of *knowing with* others. Theories of learning that emphasize relational knowing, often theories drawing on feminist epistemologies, would capture this first aspect of Nussbaum's arguments about literary discourses (e.g., Blum, 1994; Code, 1991; Gilligan, 1982; Jaggar, 1992; Thayer-Bacon, 1997; Urban Walker, 1989).

Moreover, literary texts as modes of philosophical inquiry help reveal the importance of *feeling* for *knowing*. Knowledge of persons is partly constituted by feeling; new forms of practice are connected with new kinds of feelings. In literary texts, discourses of feeling are typically interwoven with discourses of reasoning or cognitive awareness. Such is the nature of lived experience, Nussbaum argues. The tendency to split off feelings from cognitive awareness or moral reasoning mirrors a tendency to exclude literary texts from philosophical inquiries. These exclusions create a distorted or one-sided view of how subjects construct understandings with other subjects.

Finally, processes of understanding and learning involve weaving increasingly complex strands of connection with concrete others. Rather than images of increasing levels of abstraction *from* a lived world, literary texts evoke a different metaphor. As learners engage in practices and relations, they form thicker webs of connection with others. In Carson McCullers's (1946/1987) story "The Member of the Wedding," the adolescent searches of Frankie for a "we of me" (see Chapter 1) evoke what Nussbaum depicts as a view of knowledge. The early Greek image of the psyche becomes an apt metaphor for Frankie's changes. As Nussbaum (1986) writes, the process of inquiry—of achieving a deeper and richer understanding of those changes—becomes, then, one of "reading" those complex particulars, as one might engage with the concrete details of a narrative text:

> The [early Greek] lyrics both show us and engender in us a process of reflection and (self)-discovery that works through a persistent attention to and a (re)-interpretation of concrete words, images, incidents. We reflect on an incident not by subsuming it under a general rule, not by assimilating its features to the terms of an elegant scientific procedure, but by burrowing down into the depths of the particular, finding images and connections that will permit us to see it more truly, describe it more richly; by combining this burrowing with a horizontal drawing of connections, so that every horizontal link contributes to the depth of our view of the particular, and every new depth creates new horizontal links . . . . The Sophoclean soul is more like Heraclitus's image of *psuchē*: a spider sitting in the middle of its web, able to feel and respond to any tug in any part of the complicated structure. It advances its understanding of life and of itself not by a Platonic movement from the particular to the universal, from the perceived world to a simpler, clearer world, but by hovering in thought and imagination around the enigmatic complexities of the seen particular (as we, if we are good readers of this style, hover around the details of the text). (p. 69)

These discussions about literary texts are important for thinking about educational inquiries—for considering the importance of "hovering in thought and imagination around the enigmatic complexities of the seen particular." If, as Nussbaum suggests, much of what we come to know is shaped by relations with concrete others, then attentiveness to those relations may be important for shaping educational theory. There might be value in allowing educational texts to move the reader in ways similar to those in which literary texts evoke the lived and felt realities of fictionalized persons. On the one hand, literary discourses might help to illuminate the complexity of the lived worlds of students and teachers. Such discourses might be suited to the task of gaining *understanding* (which Bakhtin, 1986, distinguishes from *explanation*) of those complexities. In addition, research discourses that engage with literary texts might enable alternative ways of "reading" educational processes. Hybrid inquiries that engage with both literary and nonliterary discourses might help create alternative forms of practice and associated values. These might give voice to aspects of living and learning that have been more oblique in the languages of social science inquiry.

I turn now to an educational text that illustrates such commitments. Mike Rose's (1989) book *Lives on the Boundary* is a study of how poor and working-class students engage with the literacies of educational institutions—the cultural discourses that students must appropriate if they are to participate successfully in schools and institutions of higher education. Rose's text is a hybrid one. It moves between narratives detailing the particulars of his life, and the lives of other working-class students, and social commentary on the complexities of educational achievement for poor and working-class students. The importance of his arguments for the field of education is bound up with this hybridity. Rich details about literacies and lives are revealing of the desires and search for belonging so integral to Rose's learning experiences and to his later readings and rhetorical shapings of other "lives on the boundary." The reader is not distanced from feeling and moral complexity; the more generalized arguments that frame the text emerge in close dialogue with such particulars. It is worth looking more closely at that text to explore how literary arts might help readers to understand the feelings and relations that constitute engagement in new practices.

LIVING AND WRITING ACROSS BOUNDARIES

Rose frames his study of "remedial" education with reflective commentary about the mixed genres that characterize his writing. He is aware of the potential hazards of writing lives (and centrally among them his own life) as a means of probing educational questions; the seduction of narrative particulars can lead the reader toward stereotypes as opposed to morally complex understandings. At the same time, he expresses how movement through particulars was necessary for his own understanding of the dilemmas faced by poor and working-class students—and presumably also for his readers' deeper understanding of those dilemmas:

> Representative men are often overblown characters; they end up distorting their own lives and reducing the complexity of the lives they claim to represent. But there are some things about my early life, I can see now, that are reflected in other working-class lives I've encountered: the isolation of neighborhoods, information poverty, the limited means of protecting children from family disaster, the predominance of such disaster, the resilience of imagination, the intellectual curiosity and literate enticements that remain hidden from the schools, the feelings of scholastic inadequacy, the dislocations that come from crossing educational boundaries. (pp. 8–9)

The book unfolds as a critique of more reductive views of why some students fail to appropriate the literacies of schools, colleges, and universities—the modes of talking, writing, and social engagement that enable successful participation in middle-class institutions of learning. It critiques arguments that problems of democratic access and achievement can be addressed solely through the accumulation of bodies of knowledge (as in Hirsch's, 1987, arguments about "cultural literacy") or of language skills (as in traditional grammar instruction). Instead, Rose's text attempts to portray students' engagement with literacies as complex aspects of *lives*. Educational policies and practices often gloss over such specificity, with the result that multilayered aspects of lived experience are reduced to stereotypical statements about remedial learners and academic success remains undemocratically distributed. As Rose states near the end of his book:

> Instead of analysis of the complex web of causes of poor performance, we are offered [by canonists] a faith in the unifying power of a body of knowledge, whose infusion will bring the rich and the poor, the longtime disaffected and the uprooted newcomers into cultural unanimity. If this vision is democratic, it is simplistically so, reductive, not an invitation for people truly to engage each other at the point where cultures and classes intersect. (p. 237)

As an alternative means of engaging with such social issues, Rose's text considers them through the lens of complex particularity. Rose uses what he calls "exploratory stories" to allow the reader to see and feel more richly the difficulties of crossing cultural boundaries. His rhetorical choices lend a different shape to such issues; they support an engagement that entails "hovering in thought and imagination around the enigmatic complexities of the seen particular" (Nussbaum, 1986). Such choices, as he is aware, have consequences for the ways in which educational issues are framed by teachers, researchers, and policy makers:

> The longer I stay in education, the clearer it becomes to me that some of our basic orientations toward the teaching and testing of literacy contribute to our inability to see. To truly educate in America, then, to reach the full sweep of our citizenry, we need to question received perception, shift continually from the standard lens. The exploratory stories that bring this book to its close encourage us to sit close by as people use language and consider, as we listen, the orientations that limit our field of vision. (p. 205)

It would be enriching for Rose's arguments were he to support them through the recounting of individual cases—stories of students engaging with literacies. This is one part of the overall purposes of the text. Stories about poor and working-class students with whom he worked in different contexts support his arguments for a different kind of vision of democratic access. However, the hybrid nature of this text, the interweaving of narratives with social commentary, also has the effect of moving the reader toward what Rose suggests might be a different way of *perceiving*. The languages of feeling and moral complexity, shaped in part through the discourses of the novel, evoke for the reader the ways in which literacy practices are infused with feeling and attachment; they occur through engagements *in* a social world. The process of coming to terms with cultural literacies, some alien to one's own culture, is revealed in Rose's text to be as complicated and nuanced as Frankie's adolescent longings in "The Member of the Wedding." The details of the narrative prose are integral to readers' movement toward a deeper understanding of such complex educational issues; its textures focus our reading on a search for richer, thicker sets of connections. Images and metaphors evoke the worlds of working-class learners who encounter more than just bodies of knowledge or grammatical differences in their individuated journeys through the educational system.

> I have a vivid memory of sitting on the edge of my bed—I was twelve or thirteen maybe—and listening with unease to a minute or so of classical music. I don't know if I found it as I was turning the dial, searching for the Johnny Otis Show or the live broadcast from Scribner's Drive-In, or if the tuner had simply drifted into another station's signal. Whatever happened, the music caught me in a disturbing way, and I sat there, letting it play. It sounded like the music I heard in church, weighted, funereal. Eerie chords echoing from another world. I leaned over, my fingers on the tuner, and, in what I remember as almost a twitch, I turned the knob away from the melody of these strange instruments. My reaction to the other high culture I encountered—*The Iliad* and Shakespeare and some schoolbook poems by Longfellow and Lowell—was similar, though less a visceral rejection and more a rejecting disinterest, a sense of irrelevance. The Shakespearean scenes I did know—saw on television, or read or heard in grammar school—seemed snooty and put-on, kind of dumb. Not the way I wanted to talk. Not interesting to me. (p. 223)

This analysis early on suggests the ways in which feeling is integral to how students come to know and value. A theme that emerges is a lingering sense of aimlessness, even sadness, that Rose came to recognize as having shaped his early experiences:

> It wasn't the violence in South L.A. that marked me, for sometimes you can shake that ugliness off. What finally affected me was subtler, but more

pervasive: I cannot recall a young person who was crazy in love or lost in work, or one old person who was passionate about a cause or an idea. I'm not talking about an absence of energy—the street toughs . . . had energy. And I'm not talking about an absence of decency, for my father was a thoughtful man. The people I grew up with were retired from jobs that rub away the heart or were working hard at jobs to keep their lives from caving in or were anchorless and in between jobs and spouses or were diving headlong into a barren tomorrow. . . . I developed a picture of human existence that rendered it short and brutish or sad and aimless or long and quiet with rewards like afternoon naps, the evening newspaper, walks around the block, occasional letters from children in other states. (pp. 17–18)

Reflections such as these become a lens through which the text helps readers to discern why working-class students turn off once they encounter the cultural expectations of school. Rose recounts how he and other students in the vocational high school track in which he was initially placed protected themselves from the dissonance and pain of trying to succeed in school. Tuning out, daydreaming, proclaiming as did a classmate that "I just wanna be average" (p. 28), and resisting were safer modes of response than tackling the unknown territories of science and literature. However, as Rose writes, such resistances exacted a price (p. 29). His own weaving of new kinds of identities amid such dissonances emerged initially through some altering events in his life as a high school student. A science teacher was sufficiently puzzled by his classwork to question his placement in the vocational track. The teacher's inquiries uncovered an error—that Rose's placement test scores had been mixed up with another student's—and he was transferred in his junior year to a college-prep track. As Rose narrates: "I lived in one world during spring semester, and when I came back to school in the fall, I was living in another" (p. 30).

Once placed in a different social track, how did Rose come to engage with the expectations of school? How did he move from such a vulnerable position vis-à-vis formal schooling to one in which he was able to shape new identities, new possibilities for living, in response to literacies? The evolving narrative text considers such questions through immersing readers in Rose's subsequent experiences in high school and college. Central to the narrative are the details of how Rose came to know through his engagement with others—the teachers who became important others in his adolescent searches for belonging and personal identity. A powerful figure in his life in high school was an English teacher, Jack MacFarland, who became both mentor and role model—a conduit to worlds previously foreign and uninteresting. Rose became intrigued by MacFarland's intellectual style of immersing his students in the languages of literature and philosophy. With two of his classmates in an English course taught by MacFarland, Rose became a member of a "fledgling literati" (p. 35) interested in everything from literature to art, theater, and Hollywood bookstores. As he narrates: "I was happy and precocious and a little scared as well, for Hollywood Boulevard was thick with a kind of decadence that was foreign to the South Side. After the Cherokee [bookstore], we would head back to the security of MacFarland's apartment, slaphappy with hipness" (p. 36). Rose's text suggests the ways in which his learning was embedded in the social relations and identities he formed with others, as the literacies they practiced became part of his own life history:

> My teachers modeled critical inquiry and linguistic precision and grace, and they provided various cognitive maps for philosophy and history and literature. They encouraged me to make connections and to enter into conversations—present and past—to see what talking a particular kind of talk would enable me to do with a thorny philosophical problem or a difficult literary text. And it was all alive. It transpired in backyards and on doorsteps and inside offices as well as in the classroom. I could smell their tobacco and see the nicks left by their razors. They liked books and ideas, and they liked to talk about them in ways that fostered growth rather than established dominance. They lived their knowledge. And maybe because of that their knowledge grew in me in ways that led back out to the world. I was developing a set of tools with which to shape a life. (p. 58)

So rooted is much of educational research in the languages of social and natural sciences that some important truths about literacy practices might be missed were one to ignore the complexities of lived experience. Rose's text is suggestive of the truths that Nussbaum would associate with a love or a tragedy, the truths that might be discerned through close readings or through attachments with others. Do not such truths define all educational experiences, in ways that are as profound for our lives as anything intellectual? Are they not part of intellectual achievement itself? Rose's text suggests that feeling, valuing, and "knowing with," all part of relations within particular locations, are integral to engaging in new literacy practices. As he writes about his later experiences teaching poor and working-class students:

> Teaching, I was coming to understand, was a kind of romance. You didn't just work with words or a chronicle of dates or facts about the suspension of protein in milk. You wooed kids with these things, invited a relationship of sorts, the terms of connection being the narrative, the historical event, the balance of casein and water. Maybe nothing was "intrinsically interesting." Knowledge gained its meaning, at least initially, through a touch on the

shoulder, through a conversation of the kind Jack MacFarland and Frank Carothers and the others used to have with their students. My first enthusiasm about writing came because I wanted a teacher to like me. (p. 102)

Rose's text entails a crossing of boundaries—boundaries defined by the typical rhetorical practices of disciplines such as education, psychology, and the literary arts. This textual hybridity is part of what contributes to its importance for education. Engaging with the text, we are less able to divorce feeling and relations in the world from arguments about education. The multilayered complexity of lived experience is revealed through richness of detail, metaphor, and poetic imagery. The rhetorical hybridity of the text not only moves discerning readers toward a deeper understanding of the complexities of literacies as aspects of lives; its movement between narrative particulars and social commentary also engenders different ways of perceiving educational issues. The general commentary constructed avoids reductionisms that divorce poor and working-class students' quests for social belonging from educators' efforts to engage them in the literacy practices of schools, universities, and workplaces.

If educators want to address the dilemmas and needs of students outside the mainstream of middle-class discourses and social practices, questions about *how* we engage with such issues as researchers and writers seem highly relevant to the field. Social scientific discourses tend to keep our focus more on generalized relations, such that we can lose the particulars of the histories that give shape and meaning to engagements with literacies. If we shift our lens to social-material practices, relations, and histories, what comes into sharper relief are complex individuals who strive not only for cognitive awareness but for social belonging and identity. An appropriate ethical task, then, is one of trying to be "true to" the particulars of these histories. This is the task I have set for myself. Rather than seeking a single language of inquiry, my search has been for a hybrid language in which literary and essayist discourses intermingle. That search has been influenced by my readings of theory that addresses literary discourses and their connection to philosophy. I turn to the most influential of theorists for me, Mikhail Bakhtin, as I articulate how I read his work in connection with situated accounts of teaching and learning.

VER'NOST

When educators draw on Bakhtin's work to shape theory or research, they often cite his essays on speech genres (1986) or his writings on the discourse of the novel (1981). Literacy researchers such as Anne Haas

Dyson (1989, 1993), for instance, use Bakhtin's writings as a means of reflecting on how language practices shape relations between children and the social worlds in which they construct identities as speakers, readers, and writers. Sociocultural learning theorists such as James Wertsch (1991) describe how Bakhtin's work provides a framework for thinking about how social dialogue mediates learning. Activity is filtered through the forms of discourse available in learners' social milieus, scholars such as Wertsch argue. Socially shared forms of language provide a cultural toolkit (Bruner, 1996; Wells, 1996) that learners use to make meaning in their worlds. Identities and practices are constructed through the social genres that surround young learners. Moreover, all moments of language use occur in dialogue with others who give voice to culturally specific language practices. *Dialogue* therefore becomes an important metaphor for educators who draw on Bakhtin's work. A spoken word or written text is uttered (or written) in response to some other—a particular speaker, a text previously encountered, words appearing in the media, an imaginary listener. Because speakers or writers draw on multiple discourses in any given moment of living, and because their speech (or writing) is shaped by the response of others, language practices are, as Bakhtin argues, *heteroglossic.* They are multivocal happenings even if one is acting individually. They are shaped by the always-already social world of images and texts in particular social settings.

Bakhtin's (1981) writings on the discourse of the novel (where he writes about the complexities of social dialogue) and his (1986) essays on speech genres (where he writes about meanings and ideologies practiced through social discourses) are important vantage points from which to reflect on literacy learning. These essays help provide literacy educators with ways of thinking about how discourses in cultural contexts create the possibilities for students' engagements with texts. As with poststructuralist theories of discourse, Bakhtin's writings on language help avoid an overly simplistic view of language and identities. His work articulates a pluralistic view of how language practices mediate students' social and textual worlds. His focus on social dialogue places relations with social others at the heart of acting, composing, and knowing.

At the same time, Bakhtin's writings on social dialogue articulate some concepts that are easily lost among educators who use his essays to construct more socially situated theories and research practices. Like Seyla Benhabib, Bakhtin saw the dialogic other with whom learners talk, reason, and act as both a generalized other and a concrete subject with a narrative history. Bakhtin's essays are complicated by their own hybridity—situated in studies of discourse, studies of the novel, and readings of philosophy. An important concept that can be overlooked because of this complexity is the infusion of social dialogue with moral tones or shadings. For Bakhtin, social dialogue would be empty and meaningless without the "weight" of moral relationship. His theory of language allows space for the kinds of everyday attachments that create the conditions for response. Particular self–other relations are important to the dialogue that Bakhtin portrayed as both situated in broader social relations and ideologies, and unique to participants who value, feel, speak, and know in relation to one another. As Bakhtin argues in his early philosophical essays, a theory of acting and knowing implies a certain moral *answerability*. Without the particularity of attachment, feeling, and valuing, dialogue can have the frightening qualities of nihilism or totalitarian rule. It is detached and oppressive.

I turn to Bakhtin's early philosophical essays in an effort to highlight his concerns with concrete self–other relations. Themes of literary discourses, acts of everyday living, artistic contemplation and composition, and cognition are woven throughout the essays on which I focus. In two early philosophical essays that deal with self–other relationships, literary activity becomes a metaphor for acts of knowing. Because Bakhtin viewed self–other relationships through the lens of literary discourses, some unique things surface about those relations—things less frequently voiced in social scientific descriptions. My readings focus on how Bakhtin's early essays construct a situated account of knowledge in which the smallness of concrete relations is crucial. An important concept becomes that of *ver'nost*, or being "faithful" or "true to." I explore this as a philosophical metaphor and a vantage point from which to reflect on writing situated histories of learning.

The other is completely essential to the individuated formation of the self, argues Bakhtin (1990) in "Author and Hero in Aesthetic Activity." He writes of a subject's "absolute need for the other, for the other's seeing, remembering, gathering, and unifying self-activity" (pp. 35–36). This is a need that is emotional and valuational as well as intellectual. Bakhtin describes what in developmental learning theory might be depicted as the scaffolding that occurs between a mother and her child. His way of depicting the social relations between participants, however, focuses on the emotional shading that enables the child's individuality:

> As soon as a human being begins to experience himself from within, he at once meets with acts of recognition and love that come to him from outside—from his mother, from others who are close to him. The child receives all initial determinations of himself and of his body from his mother's lips and from the lips of those who are close to him. It is from their lips, in the emotional-volitional tones of their love, that the child hears and begins

to acknowledge his own *proper name* and the names of all the features pertaining to his body and to his inner states and experiences. The words of a loving human are the first and most authoritative words about him; they are the words that for the first time determine his personality *from outside*, the words that *come to meet* his indistinct inner sensation of himself, giving it a form and a name which, for the first time, he finds himself and becomes aware of himself as a *something*. (pp. 49–50; emphases in original)

Bakhtin is acutely concerned in his early essays with the role of the spoken word in subjects' conscious awareness. For Bakhtin, however, the word embodies not only a set of conceptual or intellectual relations, but also relations of feeling and value. What gives form and meaning to the learner's subjectivity is not language per se, but a certain kind of language-filtered social relationship. Bakhtin writes about how the other (e.g., author, caretaker, teacher) shapes an emotional and valuational context that provides new meaning and form for another individuated subject. This early essay does not deal with ways in which one subject can position another in a disempowering value context. Particularly as children leave the intimacy of home and family, the constitution of identity from other subject locations can be limiting or damaging. Even within families, such painful "bestowals" of subjectivity can occur. However, Bakhtin's work at least foregrounds the ways in which relations with others create the possibility for individualism. As Bakhtin (1990) writes in his discussion of lyric literary genres: "I seek and find myself in another's emotional-excited voice; I embody myself in the voice of the other who sings of me; I find in that voice an authoritative approach to my own inner emotion or excitement; I sing of myself through the lips of a possible loving soul" (p. 170).

In *Toward a Philosophy of the Act*, the second of his early philosophical essays, Bakhtin (1993) describes living and knowing in ethical terms. The themes developed in this second essay can be aligned with a literary metaphor from Milan Kundera's (1984) novel *The Unbearable Lightness of Being*. In the aftermath of the Soviet oppressions in postwar Prague, Kundera wrote about the ways in which oppressive regimes can distance individuals from the "heaviness" of moral commitment and belonging. A central character, Tomas, personifies the "unbearable lightness" that occurs when social and political relationships are purely instrumental means to sometimes oppressive ends. Tomas says of his repeated seductions of women that "conquest time has been drastically cut." The ironic tone of the author, conveyed in the novel's title, might be connected to Bakhtin's early philosophical writings about what it means to be an individuated self but at the same time live with the heaviness of personal commitments. Like Kundera, Bakhtin expresses a fear of totalizing systems and their associated moralities. Such systems of ethics and political beliefs can distance individuals from the most meaningful things that ground everyday relationships: the responses formed in relation to and with concrete others.

What grounds *Toward a Philosophy of the Act* is a focus on how individuals *intonate* acts of living and knowing through the particulars of interpretation, feeling, and moral valuing. Bakhtin is concerned in this early essay with the response of an individuated subject to other individuals. The kind of philosophy that can best depict experience, he argues, is one that focuses on the moments in which an individual engages in an *answerable* response—answerable in the sense that the individual owns this response as uniquely hers—and intones her response with both her own meanings and those compelled by the other. The kind of dialogue that Bakhtin envisions in this early essay is not the kind of back-and-forth script one might find in theater. Dialogue, though not yet named as such, is depicted as part of a practical philosophy that is lived by individuals in response to others. Most importantly, this type of practical philosophy cannot be adequately depicted by systems of ethics or rational objectives. What is more interesting to Bakhtin are the ways in which individuals construe contextual meanings in a shared moment of living. This enacted moment of intonation and response is what Bakhtin describes as the *act*.

Bakhtin acknowledges the contributions of historical materialism toward the construction of a more situated philosophy of practical living. In *Toward a Philosophy of the Act*, however, he critiques even the more situated historical-material theories for their lack of emphasis on what he describes as the *oughtness* of lived experience (1993, p. 20). What helps constitute practical living are the small shadings that create meaningful engagements between individuals. Without an emphasis on what he terms *emotional-volitional* shadings, descriptions of activity become susceptible to objectification. They lose the sense in which social relations are unlike the objective kinds of relations that constitute the physical or scientific world. In social relations, Bakhtin argues, the responses of individuated subjects can embrace, resist, or redefine what is given historically and culturally. Reasoning (cognition) is most rational when it is sensitive in a way that is, as Bakhtin argues, answerable.

Bakhtin, much like Benhabib (1992), frames his essay as a critique of philosophies that are overly concerned with generalized means of determining what is "good." Understanding how Bakhtin construes ethics around the particularity of everyday relations is crucial to understanding his later writings on discourse. If Bakhtin's later theories of discourse are more decentered from individuated persons, these still retain the concern with answerability that defines his early essays. It is thus helpful to unpack what Bakhtin means by answerability and how this concept for him describes what it means to be an individuated subject.

Responding, in Bakhtin's early essays, entails richly seeing. Bakhtin (1993) contrasts the kind of seeing that might be characteristic of scientific inquiry with artistic or aesthetic contemplation. In the special case of aesthetic seeing, the artist forms a felt and valuational relationship to the object of his or her activity. Typically, this object is another human subject, a center of value different from that of the contemplator (pp. 61–62). Aesthetic contemplation entails seeing this separate center of value as unique and then forming a response to it from the value position that is one's own. This kind of "seeing" can entail strong feeling; it requires more than an instrumental or objective response. The artist (writer) must, as Bakhtin writes, linger over his or her subject, coming to know the concrete particulars that are uniquely true of *this* subject. Such artistic work entails an element of compassion. The contemplator has to immerse him- or herself in the heaviness of a social relationship that is more fully rational because it is infused with the weight of feeling and value:

> The valued manifoldness of Being as human (as correlated with the human being) can present itself only to a loving contemplation. . . . An indifferent or hostile reaction is always a reaction that impoverishes and decomposes its object: it seeks to pass over the object in all its manifoldness, to ignore it or to overcome it. . . . Lovelessness, indifference, will never be able to generate sufficient power to slow down and *linger intently* over an object, to hold and sculpt every detail and particular in it, however minute. Only love is capable of being aesthetically productive; only in correlation with the loved is fullness of the manifold possible. (p. 64; emphasis in original)

Bakhtin describes in the above passage the substantial work that is required of one subject struggling to know another. That work is different from objective understandings formed outside of emotional and valuational commitments. At one point, Bakhtin describes the relationship between subjects as one of faithfulness or being true to (*ver'nost*) the particularities of one another (p. 38). He compares this kind of relation as similar to the love one finds among intimate partners. However, he emphasizes that such faithfulness (*ver'nost*) is not a passive feeling, but an active response. It is a type of seeing or understanding that attempts to encompass another individuated subject in a value system that does not diminish, or as Bakhtin warns, "impoverish" or "decompose" her. Such understanding could be described as the type of heaviness that makes it more difficult for one subject to view another purely as an instrumentalist object. It is because of his emphasis on the "heaviness" of social relations that Bakhtin construes his essay, *Toward a Philosophy of the Act*, as a project in moral philosophy. Social relationships, he argues, entail something more than cognitive or intellectual rationality. That something more is a kind of attention and response that allows subjects to be moved to action because of the particulars of what they see and feel with others.

The philosophical themes in Bakhtin's early essays evoke themes similar to those found in Iris Murdoch's (1970/1991) collection of essays *The Sovereignty of Good*. As a novelist and philosopher, Murdoch was interested in literary discourses and their connections to philosophy. She articulated a theory of ethical action that is similar to Bakhtin's depiction of responsive action. Murdoch focuses her philosophical essays around metaphors of seeing and attention. A certain kind of attention is necessary if one is to act, as she argues, lovingly and justly (p. 23). Similar to artistic contemplation, such as reading a novel, attention toward another subject requires the discernment of particulars—a slow and patient process of "reading" another's actions and meanings. Like Bakhtin, she argues for a kind of faithfulness, or, as she writes, "obedience" (p. 40) that moves one to action. A sustained effort to be true to the particulars of context and concrete others can engender actions that are more responsive, just, and compassionate. As Murdoch argues, subjects use their moral imaginations to attend, to discern. "I can only choose within the world I can *see*," she writes (p. 37; emphasis in original). Most importantly, action arises out of attachments with others (p. 71), concrete relations that reflect neither total freedom nor total determinism. Like Bakhtin, Murdoch writes of love as one metaphor for moral action. In so doing, she sometimes loses a connection with real-life situated contexts in which love is one among many aspects of social relations. However, Murdoch appears to view a certain kind of attention as a task that should engage the moral imaginations of responsible and responsive subjects. Like Bakhtin, attention and attachment to concrete others become leading metaphors for moral commitment, knowledge, and action.

Part of what defines a teaching relationship is that teachers can be moved to action by the particulars of context—of what they see in others, with others. There is, as Bakhtin might argue, a sense of *oughtness* that mediates teaching decisions. But this kind of action is more problematic if teachers cannot see the richness of children's situated histories and as a result reduce those complex histories to labels that account for children's academic failures. Institutions support those kinds of reductionisms. Lost in them are the relationships that give meaning to practices. Poor and working-class children don't just reject our discourses; they reject *us*—the others whose gaze envelops them in a destructive value context. What is required for critical literacy teaching is not just the right kinds of discourses, but the right kinds of relationships. As Murdoch and Bakhtin would argue, this requires a certain patience, an attendance. Perhaps it requires watching, living with, and reflecting over time. Teachers need support for this kind of work, but rarely do they find it. But what if critical literacy education—education that aims to empower poor and working-class children—requires the slowness of historical time, and the complexity and richness of attachments. Isn't this the underlying moral imaginary in Paulo Freire's work?

When I work with teachers who teach poor and working-class children, the first thing I often encounter is their expressions of anger: *these* children whom my lessons do not reach, and who fail their proficiency tests at such high rates; *these* parents who do not support my professional work or share my values; *this* community—and so on. What has to occur for things to change is not simply an intellectual shift, so that teachers have more information. This is not just the learning of new pedagogies—genre instruction, whole language, guided reading, skill-and-drill—or even the learning of information about dialects, cultural practices, and injustices. Rather, change also has to entail a moral shift, a willingness to open oneself up to the possibility of *seeing* those who differ from us. This is very hard work, but work that lies at the heart of teaching.

In writing situated histories of learning, I have struggled to make being true to the specificities of children's lives a central problematic in my work. My effort to come to know two working-class children as complex subjects has been as challenging to me as the task of teaching. My struggles to see the complexity of their lives, and to understand in ways that respond and enrich, are emblematic of the challenges that both Murdoch and Bakhtin describe. I grew up in a blue-collar setting, and my closest friends in my early childhood years were working-class and sometimes poor rural children. I ran around barefoot all summer, played with makeshift toys, read the few books we had around our house, and more generally acted, felt, and talked in ways that differed from the middle-class and rich folks seen on television. However, my research engagements with Laurie and Jake were still challenging ones. Now living my life as a middle-class academic, I had to cross class boundaries in order to develop understanding of their meaning perspectives as children living in worlds different from my own. The task of coming to know and write these situated histories of learning entailed struggle and reflection. This is perhaps the praxis of which Paulo Freire (e.g., 1999) and other critical literacy educators write. I see it as a task, a process, that has entailed for me the complexity of relationships formed over time. Without this complexity, along with a willingness to see and write it, such histories of learning would be meaningless: perhaps just too "light" to be of any use to others researching literacy practices.

HYBRID PRACTICES OF LITERACY RESEARCH

Much has been written about creating classroom discourses that help students of diverse cultures gain access to the literacy practices valued by middle-class society. Educators concerned about children's access to school literacies have in recent decades figured out that language has a lot to do with how children participate in school and institutional practices. Reform-minded mathematics educators, for instance, have written extensively about mathematical literacies as a cornerstone of mathematical knowledge. Teachers are encouraged by the National Council of Teachers of Mathematics (NCTM) publications on professional standards and practice to help children participate in mathematical discourses (NCTM, 1991). In the field of literacy education, a similar focus on discourses has made its way into theory, research, and teaching. Genre instruction advocates have argued that middle-class literacies need to be explicitly taught to young readers and writers, often through linguistic instruction that points out textual regularities in different genres of talk and writing (see Cope & Kalantzis, 1993; Freedman & Medway, 1994; Reid, 1987). Cultural literacy educators have also focused a great deal on language, arguing that classroom instruction needs to build on students' home and community discourses (e.g., Au, 1980; Heath, 1983; Lee, 1993; Moll, 1997). Some have described the role of teachers as one of creating instructional scaffolds that help to bridge students' primary discourses with middle-class literacies (e.g., Lee, 1993; Tharpe & Gallimore, 1988).

The starting point for creating classroom dialogue across boundaries of class and gender, however, is not merely linguistic. Rather, critical action arises out of a commitment to seeing, what Bakhtin described as faithfulness (ver'nost). This is a type of critical action that entails the close reading of particulars, a process of discernment. Children's complex histories, rather than a given pedagogical method, might be the beginnings of action. Teachers draw on their own histories as they construct readings of children's experiences. They cannot step outside of those situated locations, any more than they could read a novel or story outside of the gender, racial, class, and cultural specificities of their lives. Teaching is in these ways a process of reading—of immersing oneself in the particulars of students' lived realities and of creating new histories of practice *with* students. Efforts to be true to those specifics entail creating language practices that are answerable to concrete others. This is not simply an intellectual commitment, nor even a question of creating the "right" kind of classroom discourse.

I can remember, for instance, the first time I said "ain't" in my current work with urban poor and working-class children in a midwestern city, children who are largely of Appalachian descent. It was in the context of a reading lesson, where I was struggling with a "guided reading" (Fountas & Pinnell, 1996) format I wasn't crazy about to begin with. A little girl in the reading group had expressed her ideas using this language form, and I found myself taking up this word as I engaged in a teaching dialogue with the children. The word felt both so familiar and so strange—this hybrid utterance. I had grown up saying "ain't" and being taught when *not* to say it. Voicing this word from my childhood past as an adult teacher of literacy, I believe that I was trying to create a teaching relationship in which I, too, could cross boundaries. I knew the children would give me a lot of room to stumble as we worked on practices that would demand that they, too, give voice to words that were alien, unfamiliar. I intoned my language with the slower rhythms of southern speech, hoping to give these young readers a reason to want to know with me.

What can help teachers move toward more responsive kinds of literacy practices with working-class children? Some understanding of the particulars of community life seems crucial. This is not so much a set of general theories about "what works" for working-class children (or girls, boys, Latino children, etc.). Rather, it is an effort to learn about *this* community, *this* neighborhood, *this* family. Shirley Brice Heath's work is illustrative of how histories of place and time shape very different working-class identities. The histories of Laurie and Jake were vastly different from my own. Each educational community is in that sense particular. Some form of sustained dialogue with community members, in communities, would help teachers create more nuanced understandings of children. Understanding children's situated histories within those locations could then be a starting point for critical literacy practices in the classroom. Critical literacy as a form of social activism involves readings of situated lives and considerable commitment to creating practices that extend from those readings. Dialogue emerges from both a willingness to know others who differ from us and a willingness to imagine and risk hybrid practices and identities in the classroom.

I do not see the commitments expressed in contemporary educational theory and research as necessarily supportive of those kinds of teaching practices. Traditions of research on learning, often shaped within the practices of developmental psychology, can divert our gaze from the specificities of class, gender, and racial locations. Through alignments with scientific traditions of inquiry, they silence the voices of working-class people, of women and girls, of Blacks—those who might call into question the particular stories that are told as if they were the Gods-eye truth. In his writings about selfhood and consciousness, Bakhtin turned away from psychology and its rhetorical traditions, toward narrative and moral philosophy. He wanted to find richer and more diverse theoretical languages. I have attempted to use his work to compose new and resistant practices of inquiry rather than to abandon psychology as a discipline. I see this as a commitment that might help teachers understand that the situated histories that can lie hidden amid discourses about cognitive learning are in fact some of the most meaningful truths about learning.

Jane Miller (1990) has argued that theories can be seductive for women readers. Women can be complicit in acts of reading and theorizing that occur within a system of sexual relations. They can embrace academic theories that omit the specificity of their lives and make claims for generality that conveniently overlook differences. Miller draws on rhetorical forms as diverse as biography, memoir, literary interpretation, and argumentation as means of resistance and of creating new vantage points for analysis. As one reader and writer of educational theory, I find myself similarly engaged in concerns about forms of writing. This is not just an effort to create a more enlightened kind of epistemology, or feminist view of knowledge and practice. Rather, it is a practical struggle to engage with the specificities of class and gender locations and to critique educational discourses that reduce those locations or even ignore them.

My situated location amid theory and research has occasionally led to crossing boundaries—moving toward literary forms, then back again to essay, commentary, analysis. As one reader and writer of educational theory, I often find so-called fictional or literary texts more expressive of what it means to grow up in specific class and gender localities. Perhaps I draw on something that Susie Mee (1995), in her preface to an anthology of fiction writing by southern women, describes as a shared legacy within the diversity of experiences, values, and discourses of southern life. As she writes, this legacy is

> the act of speech—of stories handed down in which a distinctive language is honored, a language rich in Biblical and regional contexts; the love of place—where individuals, relationships, and family histories not only matter but buttress everyday life. Both are part of that rarest and most indispensable groundspring of literature, memory. (pp. 1–2)

Maybe it is that location as reader and writer, researcher and theorist, that has led me to value the relationships and family histories that helped shape the responses of Laurie and Jake to school literacies. However, I cannot imagine such things being true only of the particulars of certain childhoods; rather I see them as more generally true of how all learners come to *be* and *know*. If I turn to literature, to literary form, to evoke memory, history, and reflective awareness, it is because I have come to see these things as more widely significant for how students learn and for how educators compose theory and research. It is from the particulars of our experiences that we construct theories that are themselves practices. A valuing of history, place, and relationship is as deep a form of commitment as I can imagine, and subsequently practice, in acts of shaping literacy research.

In my effort to write histories of childhood and of literacy practices in class-specific locations, I initially turned to Shirley Brice Heath and Valerie Walkerdine as key alignments. Though working from different theoretical traditions, both scholars have, through their research, theorizing, and activism, critiqued the idea of autonomous cognitive learning—a powerful myth that has shaped and sustained not only mainstream psychology but also educational research and theory. Both Heath and Walkerdine situate individualism and learning within cultural and class localities. These two scholars—drawing respectively on traditions of anthropology and feminist-poststructuralist analysis—have placed studies of learning firmly on the "rough ground" (Dunne, 1993) of social practices and relations. Each scholar has also developed modes of activism. Heath demonstrated the possibilities of combining the study of language practices with advocacy alongside teachers and community members. Walkerdine's feminist critique of psychology and education demonstrated a different kind of activism—that of rewriting theories that have shaped and sustained studies of learning.

In my searches for languages of inquiry, I have also found myself drawn to the work of literary writers as well as theorists who consider literary texts a crucial part of their reflective thinking and writing. As I have realized, this is not just a concern about form or even content, but more an expression of certain commitments. Raymond Williams has argued that writing engages us in practices that are as morally specific as other relations in the world. As I reflected on literary texts that seem to reveal some important truths about growing up with specific others, and forming identities of gender, race, and class, I saw the value of placing those texts in dialogue with educational discourses.

Toward that purpose, I have turned to writers who have composed histories of the class, racial, and gender locations that shaped their experiences with school literacies. The histories that have informed this effort have included literary memoirs by writers such as bell hooks, Annie Ernaux, and Janet Frame. Reflective memoirs such as these recount the web of relations that shape students' identities in social settings. Students' knowings and belongings are not separated from the agencies that so powerfully impact *how* students construct identities in relation to concrete practices. The girlhood identities described in hooks's memoir, for instance, are responsive ones. The girl portrayed in *Bone Black* is not an icon (working-class, black, female) but a complex subject whose life history is shaped by a multiplicity of meanings, including those that are imaginative. To exclude those nuanced details from literacy research and theory engenders reductive descriptions of what are, in fact, complex stories— stories of being female, Black, and working-class; of growing up in the lush environment of a southern landscape; of longing for adult sexuality; of reading. Educational researchers such as Jane Miller and Mike Rose have deliberately brought such complex histories into their writing and construction of theory. Inspired by their work, I, too, have sought to create hybrid languages of inquiry.

These alignments have helped me to articulate a situated theory of literacy learning that can include such things as students' searches for love and belonging, their feelings of anger or sorrow, their agencies in response to discourses that sometime marginalize their cherished identities and attachments. I have come to view theories of discourses, literacies, and learning divorced from such particulars as reductive and silencing. They omit aspects of experience that might help researchers and teachers understand more richly the histories and relations that give meaning to engagements with school literacies. This kind of seeing is especially crucial when educators engage with the experiences of working-class children. The multilayered complexities of class and gender locations can so readily be shaped in rhetorical forms that divert our collective gaze from the relations and histories that give meaning to practices. Teaching can be reductively construed as remediation, as opposed to moral action that creatively responds to the particulars of situated histories. Perhaps it is true, as Iris Murdoch argued, that we can only change the world that we can *see*. Theory and research discourses in education are implicated in silences that preclude the kind of nuanced perception that I think she meant.

Writing itself can be a form of social activism that changes the way we see and the way we construct teaching and research practices. Writing, like living, entails shadings of experience that transform through resistance and response. To name and give shape to one's active engagements with theory can become a kind of activism of consequence to others. As

Williams (1977) argues, creative practice involves a struggle over forms of consciousness that express our evolving commitments to particular relations and forms of living:

> Creative practice is . . . of many kinds. It is already, and actively, our practical consciousness. When it becomes struggle—the active struggle for new consciousness through new relationships that is the ineradicable emphasis of the Marxist sense of self-creation—it can take many forms. It can be the long and difficult remaking of an inherited (determined) practical consciousness: a process often described as development but in practice a struggle at the roots of the mind—not casting off an ideology, or learning phrases about it, but confronting a hegemony in the fibres of the self and in the hard practical substance of effective and continuing relationships. It can be more evident practice: the reproduction and illustration of hitherto excluded and subordinated models; the embodiment and performance of known but excluded and subordinated experiences and relationships; the articulation and formation of latent, momentary, and newly possible consciousness. (p. 212)

If I could name the struggle that defines this book, it is one of confronting the hegemony of an educational system still deeply informed by the myths and metaphors of mainstream psychology. These myths construct a politics of learning and achievement that can be devastating for students such as Laurie and Jake. They distance the field from the histories and practices that could be the starting point for social action.

However, when Williams talks about "confronting a hegemony in the fibres of the self" (p. 212), this is about as real as it gets in terms of describing that struggle. In my own history, this has involved a process of coming to terms with a class-specific girlhood I thought I had to deny—to slough off so that I could be a "real academic." I subsequently spent a decade immersing myself in psychology, linguistics, and philosophy, trying to live the practices I saw as real academic work. These have been invaluable readings, as rich as any I could have imagined growing up and reading about Pegasus or tropical islands. However, recognizing the richness of a once-lived southern girlhood and the relationships that shaped it—and the importance of those experiences for my subsequent readings of children's class identities and engagements with literacies— has allowed me to articulate new forms of consciousness. Placing readings of theory in hybrid and literary engagement with class histories, including my own, has not diluted those theoretical readings but rather enriched them. There is a certain bumpiness to that kind of creative practice, an uncertainty that is a genuine reflection of struggle and change. As Williams further argues:

Within real pressures and limits, such practice is always difficult and often uneven. It is the special function of theory, in exploring and defining the nature and the variation of practice, to develop a general consciousness within what is repeatedly experienced as a special and often relatively isolated consciousness. For creativity and social self-creation are both known and unknown events, and it is still from grasping the known that the unknown—the next step, the next work—is conceived. (p. 212)

As scholars, we live the practices and commitments we shape through our texts. This is more complicated when we come at those acts of rhetorical shaping from gender, class, or racial locations that have traditionally been excluded and colonized. In the midst of struggle, however, lie the seeds of poetic transformation. My own form of creative practice has entailed a search for hybridity that I hope will enrich the field of literacy research, fostering new writing practices and their associated values, relations, and forms of consciousness. Amid those practices of writing, I look back to my childhood and forward to alternative forms of theory and practice—searching for languages of expression that will be true to the nuances of those situated particulars.

Appendix
Staff Review of Jake

THIS NARRATIVE IS A SUMMARY from 2 days of work, in which Jake's kindergarten teacher, Mrs. Thompson, and a university researcher, Deborah Hicks, discussed Jake's learning in kindergarten. Also present during this 2-day review was a research assistant, Hope Longwell-Grice. Our review of Jake's development over his kindergarten year drew upon a model for collaborative child review developed by Patricia Carini. Collectively, we discussed different categories of importance for understanding Jake: his physicality and emotional expression, his social relationships in the classroom and at home, his preferred activities and responses to formal learning, and, finally, his strengths and weaknesses as a child about to enter first grade. We also reviewed videotapes of Jake's classroom interactions during kindergarten and took note of his portfolio of work collected by Mrs. Thompson. Our collaborative discussions were aimed at developing a rich profile of Jake as a whole learner moving between the social worlds of home and school. This profile will, we hope, be of use to Jake's first- and second-grade teachers as well as his parents.

When we recall Jake's presence in his kindergarten classroom, the first words that come to mind are *energy* and *expression*. Jake expresses an exuberance that is captivating to watch. When excited about a task that he is performing, his whole body exudes a love for his work. His face easily lights up when recounting a story that he has made up or tells a personally experienced event. Jake has large blue-gray eyes that open widely as he tells about the doings of Max, his fictional dog, or recounts his adventures at the car races. We noted across the year this visibility in his emotional, affective expression. His entire body is sometimes engaged in expressing a wide range of emotions—anger, joy, often intense excitement over his own activity. His physical and emotional expression also extends to his fantasy worlds. We have seen him many times let out one of his famous "lion roars," where he tilts back his head and opens his mouth widely as he roars. We noted during our review of Jake that his physical and emotional stance in the world exudes a sense of well-being and self-confidence. He seems comfortable with himself, with adults, and with other children. The open expression of his own affect and his self-confidence seem to allow others to engage with him in a trusting manner. And yet Jake retains for himself an independent physical–social space; he does not "cling" to adults or to other children. Often during his kindergarten year, he sat at the back of the rug area during whole-class rugwork, far from Mrs. Thompson. He also maintained his own physical space during symbolic play, such as in the building blocks area.

We have observed that Jake maintains a social space as an *independent*. This does not strike us as "aloneness"; Jake does not seem socially lonely. His independence is more connected to his ease at being with himself and what seems to be a need to be in control. Jake likes to be in charge of his own activity. During the first week of kindergarten, when Mrs. Thompson called children to the rug, Jake announced, "No, I think I just want to sit here for a while [in the house play area]". Many times we observed him resisting adult attempts to structure his activity in a certain way. If pressed to do an academic task, Jake complies, but his initial reaction to a task that *he* did not choose is sometimes a quiet but firm resistance. His social position as an independent extends to how he interacts with other children during Centers work. We did not see Jake over the year form intense friendships with particular children (as we observed some children "pair up" with a special companion). He seems to maintain a bit of social and physical space around himself even as he plays with other children. During an episode of work with a large puzzle, for instance, he worked off to the side of two other children, then later moved his finished piece of the large puzzle into the work space of his two classmates. His work and play is in that sense often associative. And yet his social relationships with other children seem trusting and friendly. Even children who have difficulty forming social relationships, children whose "buttons" are easily pushed, seem to feel safe around Jake. Furthermore, Jake is not easily disturbed by more aggressive children, particularly boys, who can quickly bring a more volatile classmate to tears. We have noted the interesting ways in which Jake handles social conflicts in the classroom. He can strike out at a classmate who is really "stepping on his toes," but more typically he removes himself from a conflictual scene or simply ignores an aggressive child.

One thing that has emerged in our observations of Jake in kindergarten is his enjoyment of fantasy narration. On the playground, he quickly moves into a fictional scenario where Max 1 or Max 2 are playing with him on the playground. At times, while other children are romping on the different playground constructions and swingsets, Jake "plays" with Max: figuring out where Max is, throwing a ball to Max, even watching the trajectory of the ball with his eyes. His embodied engagement in these narratives is amazing to observe. As we noted in describing his energy and expression, his whole body becomes engaged in the fictional worlds he creates. One of us (D.H.) has seen this same kind of embodied engagement as he plays with his Sega video games at home. When he plays with his Lion King, football, or race car video games, Jake also expresses action with his entire body, along with verbalizations. He contorts his body with football hits, roars with the Lion King's adventures, and seems to get "inside" the action when operating a race car video game. Jake performed one of these embodied stories on a videotape made in his kindergarten year. When asked to tell a story about anything he wanted, Jake got up from his chair and "performed" a story about a race car going around the track. He got right inside the action, expressing movements of the car with his whole body and also with sound effects and some verbal narration. Verbal and physical expression are not things that are difficult for Jake! And yet we noted that he has difficulty putting down his wonderful stories on paper, even with his teacher taking dictation to facilitate the difficult process of encoding. When asked to tell a story about a picture he drew or painted, Jake would stall during his kindergarten year. The two-dimensional symbolic task of putting down his stories or comments on paper did not seem to interest him. This did not seem to be something that he valued, that he would choose to do on his own.

Jake seems more drawn to learning materials involving construction than activities that involve reading, writing, or drawing. During his kindergarten year, he tended to choose Centers activities that involved work/play with small manipulatives (Legos, small blocks), big wooden blocks, and puzzles. When working with construction materials—building a vehicle from plastic parts or designing and constructing a created object—Jake can be extremely engaged in his work. Mrs. Thompson described him as able to plan a design, be very persistent in his construction work, and easily find an alternative if his plan fails. Our videotapes from kindergarten show him at work on vehicles and other creations for long stretches of time, impervious to distractions in the room. This lengthy engagement with constructive materials was not as evident in Jake's work with symbolic tasks. In his kindergarten year, Jake often worked quickly when painting or drawing. As we noted, he did not typically choose writing as a Centers activity. We felt that symbolic activities such as writing were probably still laborious for Jake, that he was not developmentally ready for lots of emphasis on drawing, writing, and other symbolic activities requiring fine motor skills. We also felt that Jake's preference to be in charge of his own activity might relate to how he responds to formal tasks. If given a task that he does not value, Jake might go through the task quickly, just to get it done. However, when something really "turns him on," such as building with construction materials, he can be intensely engaged in his work.

Jake's engagement with symbolic tasks using text (reading, writing) and numbers (math) was an area in which he showed enormous growth in kindergarten. At the beginning of the year, he could not recognize first letters of words. His counting showed immature patterns through mid-year. Throughout the first half of the school year in kindergarten, Jake seemed unsure about how to pretend-read picture storybooks—how to "read" a book's pictures using some text clues. During reading time, when children sat on the rug and interacted with books, Jake flipped quickly through picture storybooks but did not seem to engage with their pictures and stories. He did not seem to enjoy pretend-reading books on audiotape when the classroom researcher (D.H.) was present. For much of the year, during whole-class choral readings of books, Jake did not seem as involved as he was with other kinds of tasks. Sometimes his lips would move along with the choral reading, but often he remained disengaged, sitting near the back of the rug area. Working with texts (reading, writing) and math symbols seems to us an area in which Jake was developmentally most vulnerable in terms of formal academic learning. By the end of his kindergarten year, Jake had made great strides: He was working comfortably with beginning letters/sounds of words, he was beginning to use picture and some text clues to read repetitive storybooks (such as *Where's My Cat?*), and he would eagerly line up to pretend-read a picture storybook during bookreading time. In May of his kindergarten year, Jake turned to the classroom researcher (D.H.) and announced with glee, "Guess what, I can read!" And yet we feel that symbolic activities involving math and literacy are still areas where Jake needs to mature vis-à-vis school expectations. We emphasize words such as *mature* or *develop* here, since he made huge strides in literacy and math during his kindergarten year.

In our review of Jake, we discussed how some of the formal demands of first grade might be difficult, given the heavier emphasis in first grade on paper-and-pencil work. At the end of kindergarten, Jake was still connecting more with construction activities (such as building things), and he was still less interested in activities using literacy. We felt that some work with three-dimensional materials would be developmentally helpful for Jake, things such as cutting and pasting out of magazines to make up a story. We had noted during our review how helpful Jake's work with Mrs. Simms, the school reading specialist, seemed to be for him. In these small-group sessions, Jake worked on story understanding using computer programs. He seemed very engaged in these sessions, maybe because the computer versions of storybooks were a little bit like his Sega video games at home! We did express our concerns about his progress in literacy during first grade. If the formal expectations of first grade are not where he is developmentally, we fear that he will "turn off" to formal learning. We discussed how Jake needs to find some value in formal learning (reading, writing, math, science). We noted how supportive his family is for him and how deeply he seems to connect with his family and home life. Jake's loving connection with his family is certain to be an enormous strength as he moves into first- and second-grade work. We "wondered aloud" whether there could be ways to help him value literacy even more. Jake currently reads his take-home "reading train" books with his grandmother, and that is a special part of his relationship with her. Could there be forms of reading and writing that connect with his interest in car racing? Could there be ways to bridge his preference for working with construction materials with his need to start writing? Could there be ways to show that we value his fantastic stories so much that we want to get these recorded somehow? Could science, given his love of exploring through materials, become an area in which he excels?

We ended with these questions about Jake's learning. We want this profile to be a living document and to engage the help and expertise of Jake's future teachers and his family in trying to meet Jake's learning needs in school.

References

Ahlberg, J., & Ahlberg, A. (1987). *Each peach pear plum: An "I Spy" story*. New York: Viking.

Anzaldua, G. (1987). *Borderlands/La Frontera*. San Francisco: Aunt Lute Books.

Atwood, M. (1988). *Cat's eye*. London: Bloomsbury.

Au, K. (1980). Participation structures in a reading lesson with Hawaiian children: Analysis of a culturally appropriate instructional event. *Anthropology and Education Quarterly, 11*, 91–115.

Bakhtin, M. M. (1981). Discourse in the novel. In *The dialogic imagination: Four essays by M. M. Bakhtin* (M. Holquist, Ed.; C. Emerson & M. Holquist, Trans.). Austin: University of Texas Press.

Bakhtin, M. M. (1986). *Speech genres and other late essays* (C. Emerson & M. Holquist, Eds.; V. W. McGee, Trans.). Austin: University of Texas Press.

Bakhtin, M. M. (1990). *Art and answerability: Early philosophical essays by M. M. Bakhtin* (M. Holquist & V. Liapunov, Eds.; V. Liapunov, Trans.). Austin: University of Texas Press.

Bakhtin, M. M. (1993). *Toward a philosophy of the act* (V. Liapunov & M. Holquist, Eds.; V. Liapunov, Trans.). Austin: University of Texas Press.

Barone, T. (1992). Beyond theory and method: A case of critical storytelling. *Theory into Practice, 31*(2), 142–146.

Benhabib, S. (1992). The generalized and the concrete other. In *Situating the self: Gender, community, and postmodernism in contemporary ethics* (pp. 148–177). New York: Routledge.

Blum, L. (1994). *Moral perception and particularity*. New York: Cambridge University Press.

Boler, M. (1999). *Feeling power: Emotions and education*. New York: Routledge.

Brady, J. (1995). *Schooling young children: A feminist pedagogy for liberatory learning*. Albany: State University of New York Press.

Bruner, J. (1986). *Actual minds, possible worlds*. Cambridge, MA: Harvard University Press.

Bruner, J. (1991). The narrative construction of reality. *Critical Inquiry, 18*(1), 1–21.

Bruner, J. (1996). *The culture of education.* Cambridge, MA: Harvard University Press.

Carini, P. (1982). *The school lives of seven children: A five year study.* Grand Forks: University of North Dakota Press.

Carter, K. (1993). The place of story in the study of teaching and teacher education. *Educational Researcher, 22*(1), 5–12.

Casey, K. (1995–96). The new narrative research in education. *Review of research in education, 21,* 211–253.

Cazden, C. (1992). *Whole language plus: Essays from New Zealand and the United States.* Portsmouth, NH: Heinemann.

Certeau, M. de (1984). *The practice of everyday life.* Berkeley: University of California Press.

Cherryholmes, C. (1993). Reading research. *Journal of Curriculum Studies, 25*(1), 1–32.

Clandinin, D. J., & Connelly, F. M. (1996). Teachers' professional knowledge landscapes: Teacher stories—stories of teachers—school stories—stories of schools. *Educational Researcher, 25*(3), 24–30.

Clay, M. (1993). *Reading Recovery: A guidebook for teachers.* Portsmouth, NH: Heinemann.

Clifford, J., & Marcus, G. (Eds.). (1986). *Writing culture: The poetics and politics of ethnography.* Berkeley: University of California Press.

Code, L. (1991). *What can she know? Feminist theory and the construction of knowledge.* Ithaca: Cornell University Press.

Code, L. (2000). Naming, naturalizing, normalizing: "The child" as fact and artefact. In P. H. Miller & E. K. Scolnick (Eds.), *Toward a feminist developmental psychology* (pp. 215–237). New York: Routledge.

Comber, B. (1998). Critical literacy: What's it all about? *Learning Matters, 3*(3): 9–14.

Cope, B., & Kalantzis, M. (Eds.). (1993). *The powers of literacy: A genre approach to teaching writing.* Pittsburgh, PA: University of Pittsburgh Press.

Davies, B. (1993). *Shards of glass: Children reading and writing beyond gendered identities.* Creskill, NJ: Hampton Press.

Davis, N. Z. (1987). *Fiction in the archives: Pardon tales and their tellers in sixteenth-century France.* Palo Alto, CA: Stanford University Press.

Delpit, L. (1995). *Other people's children: Cultural conflict in the classroom.* New York: The New Press.

Dunne, J. (1993). *Back to the rough ground: Practical judgment and lure of technique.* Notre Dame, IN: University of Notre Dame Press.

Dyson, A. H. (1989). *Multiple worlds of child writers: Friends learning to write.* New York: Teachers College Press.

Dyson, A. H. (1993). *Social worlds of children learning to write in an urban primary school.* New York: Teachers College Press.

Edel, L. (1984). *Writing lives: Principia biographica.* New York: W.W. Norton. (Original work published 1959)

Ernaux, A. (1991). *A woman's story* (T. Leslie, Trans.). New York: Four Walls Eight Windows.

Ernaux, A. (1992). *A man's place* (T. Leslie, Trans.). New York: Four Walls Eight Windows.

Finders, M. (1998, October). *You gotta be bad: Literacy, schooling and female youth offenders.* Featured address at the Watson Conference, Louisville, KY.

Finn, P. (1999). *Literacy with an attitude: Educating working class children in their own self-interest.* Albany: State University of New York Press.

Foucault, M. (1990). *The history of sexuality: An introduction.* New York: Vintage Books.

Fountas, I. C., & Pinnell, G. S. (1996). *Guided reading: Good first teaching for all children.* Portsmouth, NH: Heinemann.

Frame, J. (1991). *An autobiography: Vol. 1. To the is-land.* New York: George Braziller.

Freedman, A., & Medway, P. (Eds.). (1994). *Learning and teaching genre.* Portsmouth, NH: Heinemann.

Freire, P. (1999). *Pedagogy of the oppressed* (rev. ed.). New York: Continuum.

Gee, J. P. (1996). *Social linguistics and literacies: Ideology in discourses* (2nd ed.). Bristol, PA: Falmer Press.

Geertz, C. (1974). *The interpretation of cultures.* New York: Basic Books.

Gilbert, R., & Gilbert, P. (1998). *Masculinity goes to school.* New York: Routledge.

Gilligan, C. (1982). *In a different voice: Psychological theory and women's development.* Cambridge, MA: Harvard University Press.

Goode, D. (1995). *Where's our Mama?* Picture Puffins. (Original work published 1991)

Green, J., & Dixon, C. (1993). Talking knowledge into being: Discursive and social practices in classrooms. *Linguistics and Education, 5,* 231–239.

Grumet, M. (1988). *Bitter milk: Women and teaching.* Amherst: University of Massachusetts Press.

Grumet, M. (1992). The language in the middle: Bridging the liberal arts and teacher education. *Liberal Education, 78*(3), 2–7.

Gutiérrez, K., Baquedano-López, P., Alvarez, H., & Chiu, M. M. (1999). Building a culture of collaboration through hybrid language practices. *Theory into Practice, 38*(2), 87–93.

Gutiérrez, K., Baquedano-López, P., & Tejeda, C. (2000). Rethinking diversity: Hybridity and hybrid language practices in the third space. *Mind, Culture, and Activity, 6*(4), 286–303.

Hall, D. (1973). *Writing well.* Boston: Little, Brown.

Heath, S. B. (1982). What no bedtime story means: Narrative skills at home and school. *Language in Society, 11*(2), 49–76.

Heath, S. B. (1983). *Ways with words: Language, life, and work in communities and classrooms.* New York: Cambridge University Press.

Hemphill, P. (1998). *Wheels: A season on NASCAR'S Winston Cup Circuit.* New York: Berkeley Books.

Henriques, J., Hollway, W., Urwin, C., Venn, C., & Walkerdine, V. (Eds.) (1984). *Changing the subject: Psychology, social regulation, and subjectivity.* New York: Routledge.

Hirsch, E. D., Jr. (1987). *Cultural literacy: What every American needs to know.* Boston: Houghton Mifflin.

hooks, b. (1996). *Bone Black: Memories of girlhood*. New York: Henry Holt.

Jaggar, A. (1992). Love and knowledge: Emotion in feminist epistemology. In A. Jaggar & S. Bordo (Eds.), *Gender/body/knowledge: Feminist reconstructions of being and knowing* (pp. 145–171). New Brunswick, NJ: Rutgers University Press.

Kennedy, A. L. (1990). *Night geometry and the Garscadden trains*. London: Phoenix.

Kundera, M. (1984). *The unbearable lightness of being* (M. H. Heim, Trans.). New York: Faber & Faber.

Lee, C. (1993). *Signifying as a scaffold for literary interpretation: The pedagogical implications of an African-American discourse genre* (NCTE Research Report No. 26). Urbana, IL: National Council of Teachers of English.

Lemke, J. (1990). *Talking science: Language, learning, and values*. Norwood, NJ: Ablex.

Lloyd, G. (1984). *The man of reason: "Male" and "female" in Western philosophy*. Minneapolis: University of Minnesota Press.

McCullers, C. (1987). The member of the wedding. In V. S. Carr (Ed.), *Collected stories of Carson McCullers* (pp. 257–392). Boston: Houghton Mifflin. (Original work published 1946)

McDermott, R. P. (1996). The acquisition of a child by a learning disability. In S. Chaiklin & J. Lave (Eds.), *Understanding practice: Perspectives on activity and context* (pp. 269–305). New York: Cambridge University Press.

McLaren, P., & Lankshear, C. (1993). Critical literacy and the postmodern turn. In C. Lankshear & P. McLaren (Eds.), *Critical literacy: Politics, praxis, and the postmodern* (pp. 379–419). Albany: State University of New York Press.

Mee, S. (1995). Introduction. In S. Mee (Ed.), *Downhome: An anthology of southern women writers* (pp. 1–5). New York: Harcourt Brace.

Middleton, S. (1993). *Educating feminists: Life histories and pedagogies*. New York: Teachers College Press.

Miller, J. (1986). *Women writing about men*. London: Virago Press

Miller, J. (1990). *Seductions: Studies in reading and culture*. London: Virago Press (reissued in 1991 by Harvard University Press).

Miller, J. (1996). *School for women*. London: Virago Press.

Moll, L. (1997). The creation of mediating settings. *Mind, Culture, and Activity*, 4(3), 191–199.

Murdoch, I. (1991). *The sovereignty of good*. New York: Routledge. (Original work published 1970)

National Council of Teachers of Mathematics (NCTM). (1991). *Professional standards for teaching mathematics*. Reston, VA: Author.

Nussbaum, M. (1986). *The fragility of goodness: Luck and ethics in Greek tragedy and philosophy*. New York: Cambridge University Press.

Nussbaum, M. (1990). *Love's knowledge: Essays on philosophy and literature*. New York: Oxford University Press.

O'Connor, F. (1998). Good country people. In *The complete stories* (pp. 271–291). New York: Noonday Press. (Original work published in 1971)

Ortner, S. (1984). Theory in anthropology since the sixties. *Society for the Comparative Study of Society and History*, 127–166.

Osborn, J., & Lehr, F. (Eds.). (1998). *Literacy for all: Issues in teaching and learning.* New York: Guilford Press.

Pagano, J. (1991). Moral fictions: The dilemma of theory and practice. In C. Witherall & N. Noddings (Eds.), *Stories lives tell: Narrative and dialogue in education* (pp. 193–206). New York: Teachers College Press.

Reid, I. (Ed.). (1987). *The place of genre in learning: Current debates.* Geelong, Australia: Deakin University Press.

Rosaldo, R. (1989). *Culture and truth: The remaking of social analysis.* Boston: Beacon Press.

Rose, M. (1989). *Lives on the boundary.* New York: Penguin Books.

Schwartz, T. (1999). *Urban Appalachian girls: Institutional and "other" selves.* Unpublished manuscript.

Scollon, R., & Scollon, S. B. (1981). The literate two year old: The fictionalization of self. In *Narrative, literacy, and face in interethnic communication* (pp. 57–98). Norwood, NJ: Ablex.

Snow, C., Burns, M. S., & Griffin, P. (Eds.). (1998). *Preventing reading difficulties in young children.* Washington, DC: National Academy Press.

Steedman, C. (1982). *The tidy house: Little girls writing.* London: Virago Press.

Stewart, K. (1996). *A space on the side of the road: Cultural poetics in an "other" America.* Princeton, NJ: Princeton University Press.

Tappan, M., & Mikel Brown, L. (1989). Stories told and lessons learned: Toward a narrative approach to moral development and moral education. *Harvard Educational Review, 59*(2), 182–205.

Taylor, C. (1985a). *Human agency and language.* New York: Cambridge University Press.

Taylor, C. (1985b). Interpretation and the sciences of man. *Philosophy and the human sciences* (pp. 15–57). New York: Cambridge University Press.

Tharpe, R., & Gallimore, R. (1988). *Rousing minds to life: Teaching, learning, and schooling in social context.* New York: Cambridge University Press.

Thayer-Bacon, B. (1997). The nurturing of a relational epistemology. *Educational Theory, 47*(2), 239–260.

Tizard, B., & Hughes, M. (1985). *Young children learning.* London: Fontana.

Urban Walker, M. (1989). Moral understandings: Alternative "epistemology" for a feminist ethics. *Hypatia, 4*(2), 15–28.

van der Veer, R., & Valsiner, J. (Eds.). (1994). *The Vygotsky reader.* Cambridge, MA: Blackwell.

Vygotsky, L. S. (1986). *Thought and language* (rev. ed.; A. Kozulin, Ed. and Trans.). Cambridge, MA: MIT Press. (Original work published 1934)

Walkerdine, V. (1984). Developmental psychology and the child-centered pedagogy: The insertion of Piaget into early education. In J. Henriques, W. Holloway, C. Urwin, C. Venn, & V. Walkerdine (Eds.), *Changing the subject: Psychology, social regulation, and subjectivity* (pp. 153–202). New York: Routledge.

Walkerdine, V. (1988). *The mastery of reason: Cognitive development and the production of rationality.* London: Routledge.

Walkerdine, V. (1990). *Schoolgirl fictions.* New York: Verso.

Walkerdine, V., & Lucey, H. (1989). *Democracy in the kitchen: Regulating mothers and socializing daughters*. London: Virago Press.

Wells, G. (1986). *The meaning makers: Children learning language and using language to learn*. Portsmouth, NH: Heinemann.

Wells, G. (1996). Using the tool-kit of discourse in the activity of learning and teaching. *Mind, Culture, and Activity*, 3(2), 74–101.

Wertsch, J. V. (1991). *Voices of the mind: A sociocultural approach to mediated action*. Cambridge, MA: Harvard University Press.

Williams, R. (1977). *Marxism and literature*. New York: Oxford University Press.

Witherall, C., & Noddings, N. (Eds.). (1991). *Stories lives tell: Narrative and dialogue in education*. New York: Teachers College Press.

Wittgenstein, L. (1980). *Culture and value* (G. H. von Wright, Ed., in collaboration with H. Nyman). Oxford: Blackwell.

Index

About the Author

DEBORAH HICKS studies and practices literacy education among poor and working-class children. Her current work focuses on how gender and class are connected with schooling among children in the primary and intermediate grades. Raised in the rural Southeast, Hicks has studied sociolinguistics at Georgetown University and completed a doctorate in education at the Harvard Graduate School of Education. She currently teaches courses on literacy research and gender and education at the University of Cincinnati.